AHMEDABAD

Esther David received the Sahitya Akademi award in 2010 for her novel *Book of Rachel*. She is also the author of *The Walled City, By the Sabarmati, Book of Esther, My Father's Zoo, Shalom India Housing Society, The Man with Enormous Wings* and has co-authored a book titled *India's Jewish Heritage: Ritual, Art and Life Cycle*. Her novels are based on the Jewish ethos in India, studied by scholars, and some of them have been translated into French, Gujarati and Marathi. Trained as an artist, she illustrates her own novels. She was an art critic and columnist for the Ahmedabad edition of the *Times of India* and wrote extensively about the city of her birth.

AHMEDABAD

City with a Past

Esther David

HarperCollins *Publishers* India

First published in India in 2016 by
HarperCollins *Publishers* India

Copyright © Esther David 2016

Inside illustrations by Esther David

P-ISBN: 978-93-5029-797-1
E-ISBN: 978-93-5029-798-8

2 4 6 8 10 9 7 5 3 1

HarperCollins *Publishers*
A-75, Sector 57, Noida, Uttar Pradesh 201301, India
1 London Bridge Street, London SE1 9GF, United Kingdom
Hazelton Lanes, 55 Avenue Road, Suite 2900, Toronto, Ontario M5R 3L2
and 1995 Markham Road, Scarborough, Ontario M1B 5M8, Canada
25 Ryde Road, Pymble, Sydney, NSW 2073, Australia
195 Broadway, New York, NY 10007, USA

Typeset in 11.5/15 Warnock Pro Light at
SÜRYA, New Delhi

Printed and bound at
Thomson Press (India) Ltd.

This book is dedicated to my grandmother Shebabeth and her aide Mani for giving me city stories since I was seven years old.

For my grandfather David Joseph, uncle Jacob David and zoo-man father Reuben David, who decided to stay on in Ahmedabad and not immigrate to Israel.

They are no longer here to see this book, but it would not have been possible to write it without their understanding of the city, which they passed on to me without my knowing it . . .

The name of the house is Zen.

I went there when I was invited by an industrialist to launch his teenage niece's book of poems. This industrialist lives between Ahmedabad and New Jersey.

There was a dinner at his home in the fast-developing Satellite area, in west Ahmedabad.

Zen has huge metal doors, which open with electronic devices monitored by closed circuit television cameras and the latest security gadgets. Under the bright halogen lights, I saw there was a swimming pool on the left, as we drove past security and stopped at the entrance, where there was a turntable parking device. From there a valet took over and parked the car on a three-tier car lift.

At the entrance, the host's housemaids, who were dressed in red uniforms, greeted me with folded hands. They were very short and resembled tribal women from central Gujarat. Their uniforms did not suit their stocky bodies, as they were squeezed into their clothes, were barefoot and wore silver anklets.

In contrast, the male waiters were dressed in black suits, white shirts, red bows and black shoes. They stood at the door with a welcome drink of watermelon juice.

Standing in the portico, as I looked around, I was transported into a strange faraway land. For Zen is a house of glass.

I did not feel it there, but now, far from the walled city of Ahmedabad with its enormous ancient darwazas of stone, tall and unbreakable, I felt locked in a glass house, thick and opaque, surrounded by high walls and enormous spotlights that lit up the house and its grounds.

Zen was like an island in a fast-developing mega-city.

Growing up in the family house at Delhi Darwaza in the old city, I could have never imagined that one day, Ahmedabadis would live in glass houses.

Ahmedabad also has a rich heritage of monuments built by Sultan Ahmed Shah, buildings by legends like Le Corbusier and Louis Kahn, but in Zen I was transported into an unreal world of glass.

In the drawing room, I tried to make myself comfortable in a box-like glass chair and noticed again the ubiquitous cameras. There were glittering chandeliers cascading from the ceiling and almost touching the floor. Uncomfortable, I arranged the satin cushions in the chair.

But on the insistence of my host, Meenaben, I moved to a bigger throne-like sofa with gold upholstery.

I was still carrying my welcome drink, but hesitated to leave it on the coffee table for fear of staining it. It was sparkling with reflections of a tall, twirling steel sculpture of a phoenix. I held on to my glass till I saw a waiter and quickly gave it to him.

The walls were covered with glass paintings of flowers and birds by modern Chinese artists, which were chosen by an interior designer. Enthusiastically, Meenaben told me, the glass walls had been transported from China to Ahmedabad along with fittings like knobs and electric switches.

Meenaben insisted on showing me her house, as the young poet was dressing up in her room upstairs. I was first taken to a large suite next to the sitting room, where Meenaben's in-laws lived.

They never mixed with guests. Seeing me standing in the doorway, the old couple was uncomfortable, so they greeted me and asked me to share a simple Gujarati meal with them, a khichdi of rice cooked with pulses, and potatoes tempered with cumin and milk. Even before I could answer, my hostess quickly led me into the dining room. It was an oval room with glass cabinets, which displayed their collection of wine glasses from all over the world. When I looked at her inquiringly, she said, 'No, we do not drink.'

She had made a small change in the design, by lining the bottom shelf of the cabinet with pickle bottles and containers filled with paper-thin wheat-flour khakhras, deep-fried puris, spicy puffed rice, and chickpea crisps like sev and ganthia. The dining table and chairs were made of glass, so I assumed they did not eat at the table as they had a food lift in the kitchen.

Casually, Meenaben informed me, they rarely ate together. Everybody ate separately, while her in-laws ate at fixed timings. Very often, food was sent to her husband's conference room, where he had closed-door meetings with foreign collaborators. With great pride, Meenaben showed me the food lift. I had seen it in television shows, but this one was real and looked like a chimney attached to a cabinet. She explained its functions, 'I press a button from my bedroom and the cook sends the food upstairs in a platter, by the food lift. Microwaves are placed all over the house, so, if necessary, food is heated by the upstairs staff.'

In the kitchen there were reversible cabinets, a rotating dining table with bar stools, a huge L-shaped granite platform fitted with induction heater and cooking gas ranges of all sizes, a designer chimney, exhaust fans, wall-to-wall refrigerators, enormous freezers, built-in ovens, microwaves in four sizes, two coffee machines and, of course, the cameras.

The back door of the kitchen led to a small lawn and a garden wall, where they had a wood-fired oven made with double-fired bricks, as their chef was trained in Italy to make wood-fired pizzas. 'All vegetarian,' smiled Meenaben.

In contrast to the modern kitchen, there was a marble slab for washing vessels fitted on the flooring outside the kitchen.

Zen was centrally air-conditioned and every possible corner of the house was fitted with an intercom. At that moment, Meenaben's diamond-studded cellphone rang and she gave instructions to the housekeeper in New Jersey. I saw that her phone had the latest technology—with a flick on the touchscreen, she showed me the plush interiors of her homes in Ahmedabad and New Jersey.

Meenaben led me to the elevator leading to the rooms upstairs. But, I preferred to climb the curving glass staircase, which had been shipped from China and led to a glass corridor. I treaded carefully, but Meenaben swiftly led me to her film-set-like bedroom, which had heavy green-gold satin drapes and frilled bedcovers. A Chinese silk-scroll landscape had pride of place on a wall opposite the bed, a spiral steel sculpture of cranes stood next to the coffee table and a Laughing Buddha in rosewood sat on the mantelpiece next to a jade tortoise. Her bathroom had sauna, steam bath and many other gadgets that I could not identify. When she closed the bathroom door to show me the interior, colourful water jets automatically came on, making the glass opaque. There were digital switches for the sauna and steam bath.

On the same floor, there was an in-house gymnasium too. Yet each room in the house had chairs for pain relief, and I wondered why they needed them, as they had every possible gadget to de-stress as they ran their international empire.

Their VIP guest room was on the second floor, which had a jacuzzi, and Meenaben invited me to be their guest for a day. Enthusiastically, I almost agreed, but then left it for later.

Back in the living room, I was introduced to other guests. The women were dressed in shimmering salwar-kameez suits, flowing anarkali dresses with long, flowing skirts, or two-colour designer saris with gold and diamond jewellery.

Soon after, the young poet whom I had come to meet arrived dressed in a shimmering black silk pant suit and a wine-red scarf with a dragon design in gold thrown over her shoulders, which she kept twirling as she spoke to me about her poetry. From her accent, I guessed she lived more in New Jersey than in Ahmedabad.

Waiters served us bowls of steaming hot broccoli–almond soup with mini falafel for starters, while the buffet table was laid with platters of paneer butter masala, cashew nut curry, mixed vegetable Manchurian, dal, rice and Gujarati-style dry potatoes, tempered with turmeric and sautéed with green chillies, vegetable pulao, puris, vegetables in hot Szechuan sauce, spring rolls, a bowl of carrots, cucumber, baby tomatoes, juliennes of fresh turmeric and a stack of roasted papad. For dessert, there was warm, ghee-soaked carrot halwa garnished with nuts, bite-sized diamond-shaped kaju-katli made with cashew and vanilla ice cream served with hot chocolate sauce. At the end, a silver plate with paan was passed around, each leaf neatly folded into a triangular cone, covered with silver leaf and closed with a clove.

Meenaben kept on filling my plate, as she nibbled on a sliver of brine-soaked turmeric herself, telling me that she left all her decisions to interior designers employed by her husband.

I almost choked when grandly she showed me an empty space in the drawing room, where they had plans to instal an aquarium with marine life.

Reluctantly I have to accept that I was enjoying every minute in the glass bubble.

Yet, I was experiencing mixed feelings too, as I felt like an intruder in Zen. I was uncomfortable with the people around me and ached for the old family house in the walled city of Ahmedabad, which is no longer mine.

1945–2013 *Delhi Gate, Salat Wada, Ahmedabad-380002, Gujarat, India.*

This was my first address in Ahmedabad.

The post arrived for Great-grandfather Joseph, Grandfather David, Uncle Jacob, my father Reuben and Aunt Rachel at this address.

The house does not belong to us any more.

The present owner is bone-setter Haji Mohamed Yusuf.

Uncle Jacob lived there the longest with his family. He sold it during the communal riots of the 1960s and moved to Aunt Rachel's empty apartment on Shahibaug road. She was head of Gomtipur maternity hospital and lived there with my grandmother.

My parents lived in a small house nearby with a garden and kennels in Laxmi Nivas bungalows. But, when Aunt Rachel retired, Uncle Jacob shifted to an apartment at Gulbai Tekra in Ambawadi area and she became our neighbour in Shahibaug.

I have lived in many houses in various parts of the city since I was twenty-two years old. During this journey, objects and pieces of furniture have refused to go with me or stayed with me, like old brass pots, copper vessels, an assortment of tables, chairs and divans, along with a Freudian couch.

They have been travelling with me from Delhi Gate onwards and have found a final destination at my new address at Gulbai Tekra. But our ancestral house at Delhi Gate follows me like a shadow and has become my permanent address.

It is abstract but real, because it exists within me.

Once the house was sold, the family became fragmented. Each person made a nuclear family. They moved to other parts of the city. Some left for Mumbai, Pune, Bhopal, Israel, England, America, Canada . . .

Those who died before the migrations lie buried in the old Jewish cemetery opposite Jubilee Mills, near the burning ghats of Dudheshwar, a little away from Delhi Gate.

The graveyard was donated to the Jewish community of Ahmedabad by my great-great-grandfather, Abraham Solomon.

The most obstinate of all our belongings from the ancestral house in Delhi Gate was the dining table. It was transported out of the old house with great difficulty and refused to enter new homes of the family. With time, it had become larger, as it absorbed the load of our memories. It could not be forced into smaller tenements or apartments with doors much smaller than the Delhi Gate house. So, like an orphan it moved from one house to another, rejected by the family. The table appeared to be annoyed that it had lost its comfort zone in the old house and the family was no longer together.

Eventually, like most unwanted objects, it came to my father, as he loved antiques. But, even here, it refused to enter our house, so it was stationed in the open space around the kennels where Father bred dogs and repaired rifles before the enforcement of the Indian Arms Act in 1959.

When the dining table became an encumbrance, Father sold it to a carpenter and asked him to make a small coffee table for us. This fragment of memory has pride of place in my drawing room where I keep family photographs.

The dealer often came to meet Father and I overheard him saying that sawing the seasoned wood of the table had been easy. I think as it had been at the centre of our lives, it had softened, while absorbing our stories of love, life and loss.

Day after day, it had listened to the inner secrets of our hearts. Over the years, it had become a participant in our discussions. Its illusionary presence like a dismembered body is scattered in Ahmedabad and still encircles me like an invisible identity.

In the ancestral house, it stood in the kitchen, a little off-centre, near the storeroom where containers of grains stood on shelves, below which bags of coal were kept. A door opened into the courtyard behind the kitchen where firewood was piled against the wall for the stove. According to my grandmother, mutton biryanis and pilafs tasted best when cooked on the dying embers of a coal stove with a burning coal placed on the lid, sealed with a roll of wheat dough. Often, she warned the maids to be careful of scorpions when they went into the coal room.

The kitchen was the soul of the house, where earthen water pots were kept. The women of our house, that is grandmother, aunts, mother and unmarried cousins, spent endless hours there.

After breakfast, when the men left for work and we went to school, the women sat at the dining table, peeling garlic, which hung in net bags suspended from the ceiling, chopping vegetables, onions, ginger and coriander, while the dal boiled.

The women went back and forth from the dining table to the stove, stirring vegetables as a maid sat hunched over a stone pestle, grinding ginger–garlic paste for the evening's curry while another rolled chapattis or flatbread for lunch. Preparations for lunch and dinner were done together.

At midday, the women took leisurely baths one after another. They would emerge from the bathroom under the staircase fragrant with talcum powder and comb their hair in the coolness

of the inner rooms, braiding each other's hair and making neat buns as they waited for the men to return home for lunch.

To me, the dining table looked like an enormous room with its heavy legs and generations of old stains on its grain, which had discoloured patches. Nobody ever thought of getting it polished, as there was never a moment when the family did not need it. If we were not eating, having tea or snacks, entertaining guests, doing homework, writing letters, reading newspapers, sorting shopping bags, or cutting vegetables, it was being covered with a ceremonial tablecloth in silk or satin with Hebrew words embroidered in silver and gold threads for a Jewish festival.

Late at night, often the elders closed the dining room doors and discussed serious family matters like money, engagements and weddings, or even tried to solve personal disputes, which often led to fights, because we heard them banging their fists on the table. The only time they were tender to the table was when they received news of a wedding, the birth of a child or when they sat there reminiscing the past. The dining table had known our history, moods and emotions.

I remember that there were fixed places for everyone, as they believed in the saying, 'Eat together and stay together.' But, they did not. Eventually the dining table became symbolic of togetherness and also separation. This particular dining table created in me a lifelong love for the species.

Sometimes, even if I have not had any other furniture in my home, I have always had a dining table. However small, I have constructed it with packing cases, cartons or old steel trunks, covered it with colourful fabrics and arranged cushions to sit on the floor.

The ancestral house also had dishes, which were stacked in a kitchen cabinet next to the dining table, and a meat safe to keep milk, yogurt and leftover food. The delicate china bowls, porcelain vases and glassware from the time of Queen Victoria's coronation were kept in rosewood cupboards with sliding glass panes.

In the old house, the staircase leading from the inner courtyard to rooms upstairs was made of Burma teak. It had a similar feel as the dining table.

A few years back, when the present owner of the house dismantled the ladder to make a cement staircase, I wanted to buy it, although it was too expensive and even if I had bought it,

I wouldn't have known what to do with it. Maybe, like my father, I could have asked a carpenter to make other pieces of furniture along with a dining table for me, smaller but similar to the one I had lost.

Old wood has a certain feel, which comes down to us from generation to generation. This touch lingers on through tables and chairs, which come from old houses. They are like the limbs of an old fallen tree, smooth, weather-beaten and comforting with the layers of polish they have gathered over the years.

I identify each object with my family, like grandmother's rocking chair, great-grandfather's armchair and the dining table. They may not be with us any more, but their presence lingers on through the furniture.

A huge planter's chair in teak with woven cane work is an antique, which takes up a lot of room, but allows me to stretch as it gives the perfect horizontal leg rest, back rest, foot rest, head rest and hand rest. Recently, it started giving way and I covered it with cushions and started looking for a craftsperson to repair it, but that was not easy, as today every possible craftsperson works with plastic or nylon strings, while I was looking for a cane artisan. After a long hunt, I found two brothers, Imtiaz and Shakeel, who had learnt to weave cane chairs from their father, Ismaelbhai.

According to them, the demand for cane work is minimal. Such chairs eventually land up in antique shops, where they are redone, exported or sold locally at astronomical prices. It is a fast-disappearing craft and has an almost extinct race of artisans. Once in a while they receive calls from royal families, artists, architects, antique collectors or people who value ancestral belongings.

Most people prefer plastic strings, as they are easy to maintain. All year round, the brothers keep busy, repairing chairs, but once in a while they get an opportunity to work in cane. Although it takes twice as much time and means strenuous work, they like to work in cane as it is challenging to get the perfect hexagonal shape in the weave. If Imtiaz cuts thin strips of cane and soaks them in water to make them pliable, Shakeel passes the strips through the apertures in the wood, knotting and weaving a design.

It takes an entire day to repair one chair. When done, it looks exactly as it looked in the good old days. It is like a grandmother's lap, where you sit, curl up, sleep, eat, read and even watch television.

Our ancestral house was in Salat Wada in the walled city, where once Sultan Ahmed Shah's stone carvers lived. We could see Delhi Gate, also known as Delhi Darwaza, from our terrace. It got its name when Emperor Shah Jahan came to Ahmedabad but returned to Delhi because his elephant's howdah grazed the arch of the gate, which led to the newly built Moti Shahi Palace on the banks of the Sabarmati.

The road to the house was lined with pigeon coops, cycle repair stands, scrap shops, mattress shops where cotton carders cleaned cotton on huge stringed bows. There were butcher shops with goat legs hanging on hooks behind bamboo curtains as their bloated intestines soaked in buckets of blood and water.

The house could be entered by pushing a wicket gate in the enormous wooden doors. It opened into the courtyard of the house, used as a common bedroom on summer nights. It transformed into a drawing room late in the evening, when water was sprinkled on the floor, string cots were laid out, covered with colourful quilts and a hookah changed hands as the men sat around it. Guests or neighbours came visiting and were entertained with whiskey or sherbet, along with samosas, both vegetarian and non-vegetarian.

In the Delhi Gate house, our day started with the clanging of brass buckets, as we filled hot water from the bumbo, a traditional water heater kept in the courtyard. It was a part of Gujarati homes for almost two hundred years, but no longer so.

Every morning we fought over buckets of hot water, as there were no geysers or electric heating rods. Water was heated in huge copper pots or the bumbo. It is hard to find a proper word to describe this unique vessel, which has disappeared from our lives, yet sometimes it can be seen in antique shops or as part of the décor in restaurants. I have seen it in the old vessel bazaar at Maneck Chowk, along with a variety of brass and copper artefacts, varying from water containers like lotas, chapatti boxes, lamps, nutcrackers, locks and chains for swings.

A bumbo stands on a metal tripod. It is a beautifully designed, ornate object that is both functional and decorative, with a beaten copper surface, about three feet high, shaped like an urn with a built-in chimney attached to a perforated ashtray at the base to start the fire. Water is filled in its belly and a coal fire started at the base to heat water.

Before the day started, it was the centre of all activity and the perfect meeting place for the entire family. Elders would be drinking tea and reading the newspaper, women would be serving breakfast and we would be packing our school bags. When the ancestral house was sold, nobody wanted the bumbo. So, like the dining table, it was discarded, sold by weight at the vessel bazaar. The sale marked the end of an era.

The courtyard led to the kitchen-cum-dining area and the staircase on the right. A room with a door that opened into the street served many purposes. It was a family library, winter bedroom, guest room and night clinic as there were three doctors in the house. At midnight, when patients banged on this door complaining of stomach ache, fever or a scorpion's sting they were seen here and medication was given according to the ailment.

The only furniture in the room was a hexagonal table with a marble top, lion-paw legs and an ornate chair. During the short winter months or when there were guests, the table was moved and mattresses spread out on the floor. The teak staircase led to the terrace and a mosaic bird feeder from where we could see the majestic Delhi Darwaza.

The storeroom was always kept locked. Once in a while, when it was opened, I saw neatly folded mattresses and quilts arranged on shelves along with bags of old cotton fluff, dusty carpets rolled with tobacco leaves, iron trunks full of old clothes, vessels of brass, bronze, aluminum and beaten copper. There were mousetraps of all sizes and sepia photographs of forgotten relatives encased in rotting wood frames standing amidst mothballs and rat poison.

Next to the house, there was a stable for horses, a buggy and stacks of hay.

At night, Grandmother slept with us in the bedroom upstairs and it was normal that one of us would slip into her bed when we were afraid of night sounds like civet cats jumping over the tiled roof. A memory associated with Grandmother is of paan. After lunch, she would sit on the swing with a betel box resting on her knees, chopping betel nut or taking a betel leaf from a damp napkin on to her palm with great skill, and preparing it with quicklime, catechu paste and flakes of betel nut as she folded it delicately into a cone and placed it in her mouth. She would then make paan for other elders of the house and give some fennel seeds to us and chopped betel nut to the maids. After which she would lean on her silk bolster pillow and chew the paan cud, lost in reverie. That was the only time she seemed to relax.

Regular eating of paan had formed a brown stain on her thumb and when we snuggled into her lap, she exuded a flavour of fragrant mints.

The Delhi Gate house is a landmark in my life, as from here, we travelled around India. Recently, while sorting old photographs, I came across pictures of grandparents, uncles, aunts—both paternal and maternal—children of all ages and family friends posing against the backdrop of Mt Abu's famous Toad Rock and the Taj Mahal at Agra.

Holidays were organized during summer months when our relatives from Mumbai, Vadodara and Pune collected at the Delhi Gate home. Trips were planned to Udaipur, Diu, Daman, Matheran, Hubli, Kashmir, Agra, Mt Abu and even the Bhakra Nangal dam, which had become the showpiece of India's development.

We always travelled by train, so a bogie was booked in advance. Women started making dry snacks, washed the metal water carriers and Thermos flasks, polished the brass tiffin carriers, sent heaps of clothes to the dhobi, aired bed sheets along with quilts, and brought down tin trunks and khaki holdalls from the mezzanine.

A professional cook was hired to travel with us, and the

baggage included bags of dal, rice, flour, potatoes, onions and spices. At home, the women helped the cook to make innumerable puris and parathas in advance for the first day's meal on train. After which the cook was in control and made sure that we had enough to eat, on and off the train. To add, the men hid whiskey flasks in the baggage for a nightcap.

The tour was not restricted to our family, but extended to family friends like the Patels, Shahs and Khans, who also carried an assortment of food boxes. The art of living in a bogie was fascinating, as we performed daily ablutions in train toilets and spent days together, fighting over berths, dozing, sleeping, sitting, watching the passing scene, eating, playing carom, chess, cards, listening to the radio or just chatting. It was interesting how an entire home was reconstructed in a bogie.

Before air-conditioned trains arrived with opaque windows and catering coaches, it was a pleasure to gorge on the specialities of the region from various platforms where the train stopped; as Shah uncle, who was a prominent doctor of Ahmedabad, knew the finer points of regional food. Once we arrived at our destination, a rented house or cottage was transformed into a private hotel of sorts.

In the history of these holidays, most journeys had been trouble-free, except for one, when we had to leave for a hotel at midnight after an army of rats attacked us.

Soon, however, our idyllic family travels ended, when two young people eloped from the bogie. The boy was Jonah from our family, who had mastered the art of filling water at railway platforms during short halts and managing to jump on to a running train. In this case he jumped off the train with a girl in his arms. The train had stopped for five minutes when Jonah eloped with Patel uncle's daughter Sheila.

As the entire group squabbled over them, our bogie transformed into a boxing ring. The story had a happy ending, as Jonah and Sheila lived happily ever after, but our family tours came to an end.

Family friends became strangers, the joint family broke up and commercial tour operators took over our travel plans.

Recently, at midnight while returning from the airport, my autorickshaw passed by Delhi Gate. The light was playing tricks on me and I thought I was looking at an abstract painting, as the colours changed from mauve to pink to green. It was illuminated in subtle pastel shades and looked like a weightless form. The lighting was subtle, fluid like water, flickering, changing, intermingling, merging and changing the colour of the sandstone.

As my autorickshaw moved away from the known alleys of my childhood, I felt I was back in our ancestral house and could see the jasmine creepers climbing over the roof, where civet cats forayed at night on terracotta tiles. The closed windows made me feel safe and secure with the distant memories of known fragrances.

As the darwaza disappeared and reappeared against the backdrop of the old city, I felt it suddenly became transparent like Zen, the house of glass.

Around this time, I moved to an apartment close to Zen. It was an unplanned decision. I realized this when I shifted from my old home of almost thirty years to a brand new apartment in a high-rise housing complex, a sort of condominium. I did not know this migration would aggress my sense of colour and light. Two truckloads of my belongings were crammed into the apartment.

I spent an uneasy night. I woke up with a start to strange sounds of car horns, mixer-grinders, news on the television and Hindi film songs on the radio. Besides this cacophony of sounds, light streamed into the apartment from the glass windows. I felt the beginning of a headache.

It came as a shock, because when the house agent had shown it to me, it was sunset and there were pleasing shadows in the rooms. From early morning to late afternoon, the light filtered into every nook and corner of the apartment from the wall-size windows.

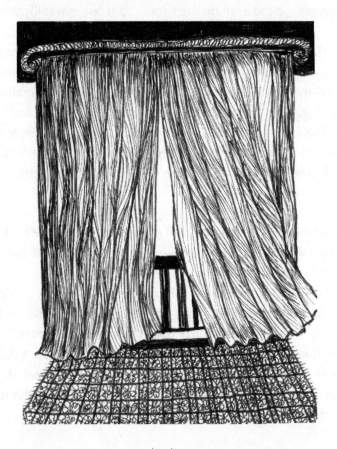

By day two, my nerves were frazzled. Yet, I held a rather reluctant housewarming party for friends, who admired my east-facing apartment, from where the moon could be seen at night from the balcony. They could not understand my lack of enthusiasm.

As an immediate solution to subdue the light, I hung up my old curtains. Then, I went to fabric shops of east and west Ahmedabad looking for fresh curtains. This meant, making detours from Rani No Hajiro to Ten Acres Mall at Raipur Gate and back to Dhalgarwad in the old city, crossing Ellis Bridge, Ashram Road, C.G. Road, S.G. Road and Vastrapur Lake.

At the end of the chase, I was so exhausted that I returned home empty-handed and called an interior designer to solve my problem. He suggested I buy thick white yardage and get it stitched into curtains. My tailor did a rush job and at midnight, I hung them up, with the liftman's help. That night, I woke up at 3 a.m., perspiring profusely as the room had transformed into an oven, and I had to take them down.

Later that day, I came down with a heat stroke and had to buy a portable desert cooler. Project Light had been shelved indefinitely.

Later, I moved to a ground floor apartment at Gulbai Tekra in west-central Ahmedabad, with a handkerchief-size garden. During this period, I discovered the world of malls.

Star Bazaar on Satellite Road has become an all-time favourite with most Ahmedabadis with its logo of an orange star, which has become synonymous with its reputation. It is centrally located and easily accessible

For long, it has been a trend in Western countries to renovate old, unused industrial sheds into studios for cultural activities. In a similar way, Ten Acres Mall was conceived on about five lakh square metres of unused mill land and built near a well-known Bhajia House at Raipur Gate, popular for its batter-fried vegetable pakodas. The road to the mall is near the State Transport Bus Terminal at Jamalpur Gate and a diversion from here leads to Ten Acres Mall, which has a neat design with a cinema theatre, bookshop, boutiques, music stores, branded jean shops, T-shirts or just curtains.

Instead of tea bags, here they serve chai made with crushed cardamom seeds and baked samosas, known as chamosa. The malls of west Ahmedabad are different with their décor of plastic palm trees, or have concave or convex mirrors, where you can laugh off your worries, as your reflection changes from fat to thin or transforms into strange shapes. Most malls have wi-fi, so they are crowded with young people drinking coffee, eating boiled corn and working on their laptop.

At most of these malls, I feel stalked as the bored attendant follows me everywhere and I dread the moment when I have to leave my bag at the security counter or allow the guard to place it in another bag, which is opened by the cashier only after I have bought something.

In this jungle of goodies families casually stroll around with their shopping carts. The children pick up biscuits, toys or T-shirts of their choice without parental consent. It is a form of family outing, less need, more habit.

Most mall hoppers shop with concentration, focus and determination. For example, earlier garam masala was used to make Gujarati chai and dal, now they have options for bhaji-pav, pulao, biryani and Punjabi cuisine.

I am prone to sticker attacks. These come in the most unpredictable of places. My heartbeats sound like drumbeats, my body trembles and if I do not make a hasty retreat, it is likely I will faint right there amongst the goodies.

Most shopaholics accept that once they are at a mall, they cannot return empty-handed. They never miss one of those special offers where they can buy one product and get two for free, even if it costs them far more than what they would pay for one.

Necessity is not always a shopper's aim. Today, the market is a seductress as she comes in the most glamorous packaging. I still prefer human interaction to impersonal shopping at malls. This is the same Ahmedabad where housewives explored the city, taking great pains to buy quality food and fabric at a reasonable price from favourite shops tucked away in hidden lanes.

The walled city is still my favourite shopping area where I can stop, look, touch, see, feel, yet not buy, as since ages shopkeepers have been welcoming shoppers, saying, 'You don't have to pay to see.'

This is where I buy cloth, foot mats, bed sheets, utensils, brassware, silver rings, fresh mint and seasonal fruit. They also have kitchenware, home appliances, handicrafts and decorative objects in brass, copper or bronze. It is known as Bartan Bazaar or Vasan Bazaar of the old city. All you need is the courage to walk in the traffic amidst the roadside vendors.

Here, women from the cowherd Rabari community buy brass pots for the traditional wedding trousseau of a daughter. For those who like to collect old locks shaped like animals or betel leaf boxes crafted like peacocks, brass water containers or lotas, bronze platters or thalis, brass chains for swings, bells, kettles, white metal lamps with filigree work, cut-outs of Om, visage of the sun god shaped like a sunflower, tridents, idols of gods like Krishna, Ganesha, Laxmi and Saraswati, all these are available in all shapes and sizes.

On the main road there is a wholesale market of steel kitchenware in modern designs, like dinner sets, masala boxes, plates, containers for storing coriander or mint, pressure cookers, bowls, lunch boxes, knives, cake moulds, spoon stands, vessel stands, storage boxes, non-stick pans and thermo-ware. In contrast, the mall is bewitching for women shoppers and we are no longer in the land of Manibens or Gujjubens. In Ahmedabad, words like Gujju, Maniben or Manibhai are now extinct.

Agreed, years back, these words were used by out-of-state big-city-wallahs for Gujaratis. We were not like Bombay or Delhi teenagers. We had long oily braids, wore shapeless knee-length skirts and billowing salwars with georgette dupattas. Older women wore longer blouses with saris draped in Gujarati style, with the pallu covering the torso. It was only during the post-Independence period that Gujarati households which held on to traditional values were branded as Gujju or Mani.

Yet, some young women did face parental opposition by wearing tight hipster saris and short, figure-hugging kurtis with churidars, like the Hindi film star Sadhana of the late 1960s, complete with hair fringe over the forehead, or Sharmila Tagore's famous bouffant with stretch pants, even as mini-skirts and elephant pants were doing the rounds in Bombay and Delhi. We still had a long way to go. Check them out in those old family albums.

We also had a language problem, as there were fewer English-language schools. In 1960, when Gujarat state was formed, the language of instruction in most schools and colleges was Gujarati, except for some English-medium schools, whose number increased by the mid-1970s. Today, English is spoken in Ahmedabad much more than before and Gujarati is becoming a second language. Most private schools are in English and offer an international baccalaureate for those who can afford the fees.

In the new millennium, the Gujju tag is no longer relevant, as most people are café-goers and look like a big city crowd anywhere, not only from Delhi or Bombay, but also they could be from London, New York or Los Angeles as they have extended families all over the world, which has made them jet-setters, and they carry off their international prêt-à-porter and accessories with élan. If the men prefer jeans, shorts, Bermudas, T-shirts and sportswear, the women are often seen in designer salwar-kameez suits with short tops, casual wear like jeans and shorts, while for parties, they are seen in specially designed silk saris, floor-length skirts, three-piece pant suits, short dresses, or palazzos. It is only when you hear them speak that you know they are from Ahmedabad.

Lifestyles and eating habits have changed. Earlier, everything was made at home. Today Ahmedabadis eat out a lot, clogging roads on weekends with their cars, which range from the latest models of Mercedes-Benz, BMW, Porsche, Audi and Jaguar to the more accessible Skoda, Maruti Suzuki, Chevrolet, Honda or Ford as they go restaurant hopping.

But, no Gujarati food please, instead watch them order paneer tikka masala, butter naan, dahi kebabs, Mexican rice, masala papad, fiery sizzlers, falafel bursting with mayonnaise, brochettes topped with mushrooms, tandoori pizzas, double-decker club sandwiches, vegetarian hamburgers, pasta in spicy tomato sauce with double cheese, or a bowl of vegetable Chinese Manchurian with fried rice or noodles, which they eat daintily with chopsticks.

Many families have a cook known as maharaj and a twenty-four-hour help; so, instead of khakhras, they have idli-dosa for breakfast. Punjabi-style cuisine is made for lunch, while bhaji-pao, sandwiches, hummus, pizza, pasta, Mexican rice, noodles or vegetarian sushi is made for dinner. Barbeques are also fast catching up, set up in a garden or the terrace of an apartment building. Non-vegetarian food is best eaten at restaurants or in the old city of Ahmedabad, famous for its spicy roadside food.

Yet, once in a while they do have regular Gujarati food. More recently, traditional food is rarely made at home, but when they feel like having a good Gujarati meal, Ahmedabadis head for restaurants or fast-food eateries, which abound in the city. This trend of eating out has inspired many enterprising women, who have made an industry of khakhras and Gujarati snacks such as nasta or farsan, and ready-to-cook packets of food which are handy when the cook takes off. These are also very popular with new brides and non-resident Gujaratis, better known as NRGs.

Yet, however modern, most Ahmedabadis nurture a secret desire for farsan, which means snacks made with wheat flour, white flour or chickpea batter, which are deep-fried and known as fafda, ganthia sev and chavanu, a mixture of a variety of crisps. Other batter-fried fritters are made with spicy vegetable fillings, like samosas, bhajias, pakodas and kachoris. Soft, spongy, steamed dhokla cakes are made with rice and white pulses while handvo is a baked lentil-flour cake, often made as a one-plate meal. Khandvi, a gram-flour roll and colocasia leaf patras are also popular snacks. These are all served with sweet-sour chutneys to accentuate the taste. Farsan shops abound in Ahmedabad and each family patronizes certain shops which are known to have the best Gujarati snacks.

There are many beautiful aspects about being a Gujarati, like the traditional chaniya-choli dresses worn during Navratri festival for the nine nights of dancing. This festival has taken India by storm and also become popular in the world of non-resident Indians in England and America. Often, it can be seen in Hindi films, but the Gujarati lifestyle has caught the imagination of television serials, which are mesmerizing viewers from Kashmir to Kanyakumari. These episodes revolve around Gujarati families, their rivalries, traditions and rituals.

Gujarat is known as a dry state, as prohibition was introduced in 1960 with the formation of the state. Much earlier, in the ancestral Delhi Gate house, crates of whiskey, rum, gin and beer used to arrive in the family buggy. The kitchen was always stocked with sodawater bottles, lemonade, Angostura bitters, along with drinks like kaju feni from Goa, mahuda from Madhya Pradesh and kesar-kasturi from Rajasthan. Every evening the glasses were washed, polished with a muslin cloth and kept ready, sparkling and clean, for the much-awaited pre-dinner drink, almost always served with peanuts and samosas.

Even with prohibition, most parties in Ahmedabad are incomplete without vodka or whiskey. It is fashionable to have a drink and talk about the latest cars, a newly built farmhouse on S.G. Road and trips to Bali, Dubai, Turkey, Los Angeles, London, Singapore, Switzerland and New Jersey.

More than six hundred years old, Ahmedabad is now transiting to a new phase, one in which the corporate world with its international industrial estate that is coming up in the suburbs plays a significant part. Once in a while, there are police raids on farmhouses around Ahmedabad, where they haul crates of liquor bottles and embarrass the partygoers, who could be enjoying an artificial rain dance dressed in skimpy clothes.

Sometimes, the media carries photographs of bulldozers destroying bottles of smuggled foreign liquor, even as spurious liquor is brewed in slums and shanties of the city and distributed in plastic pouches, often leading to the death of a large number of people. Most liquor suppliers are men, who have secret code numbers and addresses for transporting bottles, while sometimes women are also known to run this business and are endearingly called aunty or maasi, although there is nothing soft about the work that they do.

Most Ahmedabadis have always had family elsewhere in the world. Their children study abroad and a large number have become world travellers. Even if they avoid Gujarati snacks at home, they make sure that Indian food is served on group tours. More recently, when abroad, if not heading for bakeries or international fast-food outlets, they are experimenting with international cuisine and have learnt to survive on pasta, salads, couscous, hummus, pita, falafel and, of course, pizza. Often, they carry home-made food in their bags, which stays for a month, and once in a while, you will meet somebody who was a hard-core vegetarian but started eating chicken abroad and eventually became a non-vegetarian. As an added advantage, their taste buds have become habituated to Parmesan cheese, Mozzarella, oregano and basil. It is fashionable to grow herbs in kitchen gardens of most farmhouses in the city.

The boom of industry in Ahmedabad has created a new breed, known as New Money. Their lifestyle is different as most have foreign collaborators, even if it is an animal help foundation; non-governmental organizations (NGOs) with links abroad abound in the city. At New Money parties, French, German or Dutch is often heard and in many families it is a matter of pride to have a foreign bride from America or another Western country.

And, when it comes to culture, the much-travelled Ahmedabadi has developed the capacity to attend every possible concert, be it ghazals, Sufi music, jazz, rock, pop, folk fusion or Bollywood item numbers. At parties, a disc jockey (DJ) is a must, complete with a drone camera whirring over the venue. It is a mystery to me, how everything is a matter of enjoyment, as they make a stampede for tickets or free passes.

Yet, one can still find a few families that have held on to a traditional lifestyle with the swing as the centre point of their

homes. Some of these are families which owned textile mills in the city.

Then, the air was always thick with cotton dust, which settled like a heavy smog over the city and the silhouette of the city was lined with tall chimneys, which have now disappeared. The chimney of Calico Mill on the bank of the Sabarmati stands testimony to this era.

These mill owners are still synonymous with Ahmedabad's cultural heritage. Some were philanthropists who donated large amounts in the creation of major educational institutes and invited the world's greatest architects to the city, giving us the great architectural marvels of Le Corbusier and Louis Kahn.

Old Money people have almost always been mill owners, but after the 1984 mill workers' strike in Mumbai, most mills closed down there and in Ahmedabad. During this time, weaving factories and printing houses mushroomed in Gujarat, making a further dent in the textile industry of Ahmedabad.

Since 1986, Kailashsinh Chauhan has been photographing closed textile mills. He looks like an unlikely photographer, dressed in a crumpled shirt and loose trousers. When the mills were functioning in Ahmedabad, it was known as the Manchester of India and Kailshsinh had a paan shop at the Saraspur crossroads, where mill workers stopped and exchange notes and unburdened themselves. As a rule, Ahmedabadis like to meet at tea stalls or paan shops, where they also watch cricket matches on small television sets installed by the owner.

During this period Kailashsinh made some lifelong friends; he heard their stories and even became a mill worker, but he did not like the musty atmosphere. Soon, when the mills closed down, he started photographing them, with a camera bought from his savings, and developed the pictures at a photo studio. He displayed the pictures in his paan shop and only close

friends knew that he was a photographer. Sometimes, if he had a technical problem, he took advice from members of a photographers' club. They organized an exhibition of his photographs at the Ahmedabad Textile Mills Association building, which was designed by Le Corbusier. The photographs were a tribute to the mill workers who had been jobless for years, facing dire poverty till they found work as autorickshaw drivers, labourers or watchmen.

Once the mills closed down, Saraspur crossroads was no longer good for business, so Chauhan started Sangam Paan House at Raipur crossroads, where he displays his photographs amidst betel leaves wrapped in a damp cloth, a clay pot of drinking water and bottles of mints.

Even though he had no training in photography or background in art, he felt a strong need to document the mills before they were forgotten. Cycling around Ahmedabad with his precious camera, Kailashsinh photographed mills with names like Bordi, Batata, Biladi, Mirchi, Topi, Jupiter, Cotton, Jehangir, Rustom, Lal, Motilal, Arbuda, Himadri, Vikram, Hutheesing, Srinagar, Bihari, Rohit, Kaiser-e-Hind, Bharat-Vijay and Swadeshi.

This exhibition was inaugurated by a descendant of Ranchhodbhai Chhotalal as he had started the first textile mill of Ahmedabad during the Depression of 1930. A large number of Indians were boycotting cloth made in England as Mahatma Gandhi's Swadeshi movement caught on and the seths of Ahmedabad, as the mill owners were known, formed the Swadeshi League to produce affordable fabric.

Textile mills and their chimneys are almost forgotten today and Ahmedabad no longer wakes up to the sound of sirens, smog or cotton dust.

If you are ever at Raipur Chakala near Chikhaliya Mahadeva Mandir, look out for Passport Hanuman in Desai Ni Pol, a very narrow street, where even a Nano car can be stuck at the entrance.

A Pol is like a cool, shaded lane, as the close proximity of the houses does not allow direct sunlight to fall in a Pol house, which is a typical architectural form of Ahmedabad. Known as vernacular architecture, Pol houses are typical residential areas in the walled city, where people live in close proximity to each other like one big family.

Pols look like densely packed clusters of continuous rows of houses flanked by narrow streets, known as khadkis, dehlis and mohallas. It is said that they are closely connected and one can cut across the entire walled city by jumping over the roofs, which are also known as escape routes as when miscreants are chased by the police.

Desai Ni Pol has an old-world charm, as these tall but narrow houses have a wooden façade, brackets, and balconies carved with motifs of birds, animals, dancing nymphs and guardians installed at the entrance. The main door is almost always open and leads to an open-to-sky courtyard, which has a swing and is the central living space of the family. Narrow staircases of wood lead to the rooms upstairs, which are small, cool and comfortable. And, if cows are not seen in west Ahmedabad, they are still part of Pol life, as they are fed leftovers and it is not uncommon to see the pious collecting cow pee in their palms as a form of worship.

The entrances of most Pols have a Mohalla Mata, a mother goddess, who protects the Pol against the evil eye, like the one at Chandla-Ol near Fernandez Bridge, which is a marble portrait of the goddess installed in an alcove. Earlier, people of different communities lived in close proximity, but lately, the old iron gateways between Pols have been repaired, so that they can be closed to form a demarcation line between communities.

The temple of Passport Hanuman is deep inside the Pol, before Akha Bhagat No Khancho with the life-size bronze statue of the silversmith-poet Akho born in AD 1600 who lived here. This road leads to Passport Hanuman, conspicuous with a Shivalinga and Nandi at the entrance. It is believed that Lord Hanuman, ardent devotee of Lord Rama, flew to Sri Lanka in search of Sita, sans passport, sans visa, sans airport, sans aeroplane, so he is the perfect diety for matters related to flying.

According to the Ramayana, when Laxman was injured, Hanuman flew to the Himalayas in search of the medicinal plant Sanjivani and returned carrying the mountain in his hand. So, it is a matter of plain logic that Hanuman is connected with air travel, and an appropriate choice for Gujaratis, who have always been known to be world travellers.

Saturday is Hanuman's day, so the temple is open all day and prospective fliers with travel papers in hand wait in long queues for the moment when the Lord will fulfil their dollar dreams. It is said that their wishes are almost always granted. The procedure of receiving Lord Hanuman's approval is novel, as after the arti, the pujari holds the passport close to Lord Hanuman's eyes, so that he reads the details and stamps it with a spiritual visa. The devotee then makes a donation and offers flowers at the temple. About a thousand aspirants queue up at the temple, also known as Miracle Maruti, Temple of Miracles, Visa-wallah Hanuman, Chamatkarik Dholeshwar Mahadeva Nu Mandir, Chamatkarik Shri Hanumanji Na Charan or just Passport Hanuman.

Often, I went to Desai Ni Pol with my rakhi brother, DJ. It was their ancestral Pol house, where they celebrated Uttarayan by flying kites on the terrace. They did not live there, but used it to celebrate festivals with relatives and friends.

D.J. Shah was my rakhi brother. We met once a year on Raksha Bandhan day. The fragile silk thread of a rakhi, which a sister ties on her brother's wrist, bonded us. We were not related, but grew up together in Laxmi Nivas compound on Shahibaug road. We no longer live there. We have crossed the bridges over the Sabarmati and moved on to west Ahmedabad.

We had to leave Laxmi Nivas, as the land was on a hundred-year lease, which ended in 1979. The owners sold the land to the Swaminarayan sect. Each tenant received financial compesation to vacate their homes.

DJ lives on Satellite Road. His mother, Lilavati-kaki, almost ninety years old, sits at the window in her traditional Gujarati sari bending over a crotchet tablecloth. She welcomes me with a smile and informs me that she likes to work near the window from where the light floods into the house. Her daughter-in-law, Mita makes tea for us, as Lilavati-kaki shows me a sari she embroidered for herself. Her eyes are still sharp. I look around the room and recognize some objects from the old house, a marble bust, sculpted in the British academic style, a Pichwai or cloth painting of Lord Krishna, and a mirrored cupboard which has a faded painting of goddess Laxmi. Back to the present—the fragrance of freshly baked lentil cake, handvo and masala tea hits me. Mita, a childhood friend, is married to DJ. She calls me into the kitchen, where we sit at the dining table talking about how we used to sit cross-legged on the mosaic floor of their majestic drawing room eating thepla, spicy bottle gourd and flatbread with sour-sweet mango pickle.

In the 1950s, when the joint family broke up, my parents left the Delhi Gate house and lived in a rented house in the compound of Laxmi Nivas on Shahibaug Road, not far from the ancestral Delhi Gate house on the road, which led to the governor's residence, the Raj Bhavan, also known as Moti Shahi Palace, much before Gandhinagar became the capital of Gujarat.

Laxmi Nivas was a residential complex built around a bungalow belonging to Jaswant-kaka and Lilavati-kaki. It was built in the colonial style with pillars shaped like nymphs carrying flame-shaped lamps. It had hexagonal rooms, and balconies, mosaic-tiled terraces, stairways, chandeliers and mirrored halls. The houses had an orchard with tamarind, chikoo, guava and pomegranate planted around ornate fountains. Like all old bungalows and havelis, they also had a chabutra or bird feeder, a traditional architectural form of Gujarat, built on a column, with an open canopy supported by carved brackets. Chabutra rhymes with the Gujarati word kabutra meaning pigeons or birds in general. From a distance a chabutra looks like a citadel with intricate carvings of flowers, birds, animals, creepers and nymphs.

Ahmedabad has always been a nature-friendly city and each area had a chabutra where grain and water were fed to birds as a form of piety during the long summer months. This tradition still continues. It is a common sight to see shopkeepers from these areas scattering grain around chabutras for the birds, big and small, which gather there. New bird feeders are copies of old chabutras and made in coloured cement with funds received from religious organizations in memory of philanthropists or political leaders.

Then, people of all communities lived in Laxmi Nivas compound. No comments were ever made about food habits of non-vegetarian families and we celebrated almost all festivals together. Today, as I drive past a mall where Laxmi Nivas once stood, I cannot recognize it.

In the late 1970s, the residents of Laxmi Nivas went their separate ways, but kept in touch. Whenever we met, there was a certain feeling of timelessness as we transformed into one big family all over again.

In the Laxmi Nivas compound, Mita and Pratibha were my best friends. Sometimes, I used to eat with their families and it was an education to learn the subtleties of traditional Gujarati cuisine. It was here that I first saw a huge sev-making machine. A perforated tray was filled with chickpea paste and placed over an enormous round-bottomed two-handled cast-iron karhai of hot oil. As the machine was cranked, strands of vermicelli-like sev was deep-fried, lifted on a slotted spatula, placed in a huge basket, cooled and packed in airtight boxes. Then, snacks were prepared at home. No longer so. Mostly they are bought off the rack from malls or speciality shops, usually run by women.

During summer, pickles like choondo and gorkeri were made at home. It is amazing how a small jar of pickle can make one nostalgic about old times. Normally, whenever old houses are sold, the unused lidded ceramic pickle jars are given away to maids or scrap dealers.

It is interesting to note how some people keep them as part of the décor, while others use them as flowerpots. Each jar was like a storehouse of family histories. Interestingly, new jars with old brand names from north Gujarat are still available at Teen Darwaza.

The main bungalow at Laxmi Nivas had an enormous mosaic chowk with floral patterns. It was where DJ's younger sister Pratibha taught me how to fly my first kite during Uttarayan. She also lent me her chaniya-choli dress and I learnt my first steps of garba dance during Navratri. Around that time, DJ took to eating omelettes with my father. It was an enchanting childhood, where there were no barriers between vegetarians and non-vegetarian families.

Diwali has a special meaning for me, as my childhood was spent in the walled city of Ahmedabad. According to legend, Goddess Laxmi lives here and visits our homes on Diwali night, when we make the most beautiful rangolis, light clay lamps and welcome her.

This idea captured my imagination from a very young age, and walking in the old city, I often wonder if I will see her, maybe, in the alcove of the Teen Darwaza, where an eternal light is kept burning for her, to show that she is in Ahmedabad. For this very reason, some old-timers retain their old shops here, even if they have large establishments in malls of the fast-developing west Ahmedabad.

I like to remember the many Diwalis celebrated in the past with friends, like the last day of Navratri, when we folded and stored away those sexy backless cholis, ruefully worn once a year, along with the embroidered skirts and sequined half-saris. We did not have to buy passes to participate in festivities, but today, garbas are held in party plots or clubs, where each pass comes for a price.

In contrast, the festivities of my childhood days were friendly and affectionate, as women spent hours making snacks and sweets and cajoled each other to taste the delicacies, exchanging recipes and even proclaiming that a certain 'behn' made the best snacks, without a trace of envy. It was a warmth which entered our homes and hearts. With changing lifestyles as people move to high rise condominiums and gated societies that are spreading octopus-like on S.G. Highway, Diwali has become more insular and the community feeling is disappearing. More so, with the availability of everything off the rack—from snacks

and sweets to strings of plastic flowers and electric lights. There is no time to make snacks, buy the flowers, or roll the wicks for the clay lamps.

The women used to dress in traditional Gujarati saris and greet each other with platters of sweets and snacks arranged in a thali, covered with an embroidered cloth during Diwali. This simple act was like an offering of love and greetings for the New Year, but it has now been overtaken by corporate gift boxes of chocolates or nuts, which arrive at your doorstep by courier.

As you graciously accept the gift and put it away, a simple word surfaces in the mind—'sabras', when on New Year, early

in the morning, children went from house to house with platters of rock salt, which they gave us in return of a few coins, much to their delight.

As Laxmi Nivas stood on the road to Raj Bhavan, we sometimes saw the governor as he drove past in an open Buick car with visiting dignitaries like Prime Minister Jawaharlal Nehru. The car would drive past slowly, stopping often, as bouquets of roses were offered to the dignitaries, which they accepted graciously, often giving the flowers back to the children standing in rows along the road. Here, we also saw Queen Elizabeth II, who visited Ahmedabad in 1961, and we were thrilled when she waved at us with her gloved hands. But it was even more exciting to see the American ambassador to India, J.K. Galbraith, as he stood in the car, waving at us like a palm tree lodged in a tiny boat, as he was very tall. I had read in the newspapers that a room in Raj Bhavan had been renovated befitting the queen of England and later a new bed had to be custom-made for Galbraith in 1963, so that he could fit into it.

Gujarat became a state on 1 May 1960, after it split up from Maharashtra. Ahmedabad became the capital of Gujarat and the first governor was Mehdi Nawaz Jung from the royal family of Hyderabad. Moti Shahi Palace became his official residence, where he met dignitaries and hosted banquets for well-known people of Ahmedabad, or just invited Urdu poets in the Diwan-e-Khas, the main hall of the palace, which had an open terrace overlooking the Sabarmati.

In 1978, the governor's residence was shifted to Gandhinagar. The palace was allotted to the Sardar Vallabhbhai Patel Memorial Society in 1979. It was no longer listed as a heritage building by the Archaeological Survey of India. Soon after, the mirrors and chandeliers disappeared; instead, photographs of Patel's life were displayed in the Diwan-e-Khas. In 2012, the palace was in a run-down condition till the trustees of the society decided to break down some parts to modernize it.

Long back, in 1622, Emperor Shah Jahan planned a huge garden around the palace, constructing porches, seats, towers, wells and canals which ran around it. Resevoirs were dug for the upkeep of the gardens surrounded by a small rampart wall. An avenue within the garden led to the royal palace. It had a large staff to maintain the garden. With time, the garden disappeared, yet the entire area was known as a royal garden, Shahibaug.

Malav had never heard about the palace, but when he read about it in the newspapers, he was curious. He is a thirty-something computer engineer and whenever we meet, he tells me with a certain amount of pride that he rarely goes to the old city. He avoids it even when he has to reach the airport. To avoid this route, he often takes a circular route from Gandhi Ashram to Subhash Bridge leading to Shahibaug underbridge and to the airport.

While he repairs my laptop, he asks me questions about the walled city. My answers confuse him and I can never convince him about its finer points. I tell him, the walls are now mere illusions and the walled area is more like a city of ancient gates separated by buildings and shopping centres. The last wall in Khanpur, opposite Cama Hotel, is symbolic of the walled city. It was crumbling, but now it is being renovated and trees are being planted along its periphery. Whenever I am in the walled city, it is like reliving my childhood. I like its density, the friendliness of the shopkeepers as they smile and offer tea, even if it is fifty-fifty cutting or sharing. I also like the fragrances emitting from the walled city, like the ones from Bhatiyar Gully with its roadside eateries.

Rani No Hajiro is a colourful place with its textiles and seasonal fruit, like mango, strawberry, chikoo, guava, papaya, musk melon, watermelon, gooseberry and water chestnut, along with freshly harvested green millet or wheat, known as ponk.

Malav often asks me to explain the difference between shopping in the old city and new. It surprises him when I tell him that I can buy everything in the old city at a reasonable price from my regulars, but I prefer cinema theatres at multiplexes of west Ahmedabad. I like the freedom it has given me to watch films all alone and undisturbed.

Yet, the walled city can be termed as the real Ahmedabad. It is unique with its division of markets, like the vegetable market at Maneck Chowk, Bartan Bazaar, the Dhalgarwad bed sheet market and Rani No Hajiro, with its shops of silver ornaments, fragrant mints, sweets, silk-thread garlands, hardware, brocade borders and hand-stitched account books. This road leads to an underpass where you can find rudraksha seeds, cowrie shells, lacquer objects, prayer beads, wedding cards and second-hand textbooks.

The cloth market of Ratan Pol is in the opposite lane. The planning of these bazaars is well defined and I often advise Malav to put on his jogging shoes and discover Ahmedabad. In a way, it has twin cities, an old city in the east and the other on the west, across the Sabarmati.

There are five major bridges connecting the city. Ellis Bridge was built in 1895 by Rao Bahadur Himmatlal Engineer, then working for the Public Works Department of the city. He

designed the bridge as a series of metal arches, after the earlier wood structure, known as Lakadiya Pul, was destroyed in the floods of 1875. The new bridge was named after Sir Herbert Ellis, commissioner of Ahmedabad. A few years back it was renamed Swami Vivekananda Bridge and a bronze statue of the Swami was installed on the Ashram Road.

The city's foundation stone is at Maneck Burj, across the bridge in east Ahmedabad. Other bridges are named after Mahatma Gandhi, Jawaharlal Nehru, Subhash Chandra Bose, and Sardar Vallabhbhai Patel.

Both east and west Ahmedabad are different in character. The walled city, sans walls, has enormous gates, mosques, narrow Pols, old houses, mosques, dargahs, temples and havelis with intricate wood carvings.

Often, I stand enraptured at Khamasa Circle in the old city, listening to temple bells ringing alongside the call of a muezzin, as people of all communities pray at their respective places of worship. The city across has high-rise concrete and glass malls, multiplexes, flyovers, Ring Roads, BRTS or Bus Rapid Transport System, restaurants, residential buildings, condominiums, newly built temples, public gardens, swimming pools, art galleries, bookshops, international schools, sports complexes, farm houses et al.

It is a city of contrasts. Newcomers to the city often complain about jaggery in the food, cows on the roads, stray dogs and the chaotic traffic. But all complaints end during Navratri or the

famous nine nights of dancing, when the city becomes truly Gujarati, as people join garba classes, buy Navratri dresses from the night market at Law Garden or designer shops as they prepare to attend garba events at the most expensive clubs on the Sarkhej–Gandhinagar Road or S.G. Road on the western highway, where prizes are given to the best dancers or best-dressed couple. This is also when non-resident Gujaratis from abroad descend upon the city with foreign guests. So far, the city is known to be safe for women, and young people are allowed the freedom of being out all night.

The Ahmedabad Municipal Corporation has decided to promote the old city as a world heritage city, so it is fashionable for locals from west Ahmedabad to take an early morning or late night heritage walk. They discover the city like tourists and try to understand its history from the times of Sultan Ahmed Shah, the Marathas, the feudal lords of the African Siddi community of Gujarat and Moghul emperors who ruled over the city.

The old city is where most business houses have their roots. Some have moved to west Ahmedabad. They have branches, which cater to foreign markets, with a variety of products like Indian sweets, spices, textiles or machines. Its residents include skilled workers like electricians, plumbers and carpenters, who work in the Middle East for a few years and return back to lead a prosperous life in Ahmedabad. Most commercial houses still function from the walled city.

There are many stories about the existence of Goddess Laxmi in Ahmedabad. It is said, late one night, when the goddess stood at the main entrance of the city at Teen Darwaza and knocked on the massive gates, the guard, Khwaja Siddiqui, allowed her to

enter, left her there, locked the door from inside and went to the palace, to take permission from the sultan. He was beheaded for leaving the goddess standing at the gate. The sultan rushed to welcome the goddess, but by then she had disappeared into the city. Another version of this story is that the sultan deliberately beheaded the guard so that Laxmi could not leave the city as the gates were locked and she had to stay back in the city. There is also a third version that Goddess Laxmi was already in the walled city, but wanted to leave at midnight and requested the guard to open the doors.

Siddiqui realized that if she left, the city would lose its prosperity. So he asked her to wait, saying, he had to take the sultan's permission. He rushed to the sultan and requested to be beheaded, because, if he did not return to open the gate, the goddess would stay back in Ahmedabad, and according to legend, she did.

Jabbar Mirza comes from a family of caretakers of Laxmi's lamp, which has been kept burning in an alcove at Teen Darwaza. He continued the tradition till he died in 2013. Now, his family looks after the lamp.

Shopkeepers believe that even if recession sets in, it will never affect them because of Goddess Laxmi's presence in the city. The city abounds in success stories. Like that of the man who went pedalling washing powder house to house on his bicycle and eventually became one of Gujarat's most iconic industrialists. There are many such tales of small beginnings which led daring men to great enterprises.

Over the years, Ahmedabad has become a major art destination, largely because of the efforts of painter Ravishankar Raval, fondly known as Kalaguru. Around the time the Bengali architect Suren Kar was designing Retreat, the Sarabhai mansion, Pulin Kumar Dutt was teaching painting to the children of the family. Rabindranath Tagore came to Ahmedabad in 1878, when he was just about seventeen years old, and wrote his famous story 'Hungry Stones' in Moti Shahi Palace. He often came to Ahmedabad and left his imprint on the art scene with his mere presence.

In 1938, on Mahatma Gandhi's insistence, Nandalal Bose of the Bengal revivalist movement and Raval of the Gujarat Chitra

Kala Sangh painted together at Haripura on the banks of the Tapti, near Bardoli, which was the venue of the annual meeting of the Indian National Congress in 1938. Besides being influenced by the Tagores, Santiniketan and the Bengal revivalist movement, Raval was also influenced by Raja Ravi Varma's religious oleographs, which were to be seen in most Gujarati homes.

During the early 1900s, Raja Ravi Varma visited Ahmedabad and painted many portraits of industrialists like Chinubhai Madhavlal and Ambalal Sarabhai, who as a young boy gave him a sitting for a portrait. Deeply impressed with Tagore's ideology of informal open studios, Raval conceived the Gujarat Chitra Kala Sangh in his own house and encouraged young people to take to art. The response was overwhelming. Raval is best known for his paintings based on litterateur K.M. Munshi's novels and the painting of Mahatma Gandhi's trial on a charge of sedition, which was held on 18 March 1922 in the Circuit House at Ahmedabad. In fact it was Gandhiji who reinforced the links between Santiniketan and Chitra Kala Sangh. Later Raval met Tagore's nephew Abanindranath, founder of the Bengal School of Art; so Raval's students often finished their education at Santiniketan. Ravishankar's friendship with well-known editor Bachubhai Ravat led to the publication of the art magazine *Kumar*, which was a household name and influenced the taste of its readers. One of Raval's students, Chaganlal Jadav, gave quite another dimension to the Ahmedabad art scene, as he was influenced by Impressionism and the modern art movement, which was also in vogue in Vadodara's Faculty of Fine Arts at the Maharaja Sayajirao University. It was the beginning of migrations in the arts between the two cities. By then the National Institute of Design in Ahmedabad had already become one of the foremost design schools of the country, with its concept of functional art. The latest addition is the National Institute of Fashion Technolology. In a state which was known for its textile industry, this institute fulfils a great need as it offers know-how and trained designers to the garment industry. The institute works around the concept of design that is Indian yet global, keeping in mind tradition, innovation and the latest technology.

Be it Sam Pitroda, Lord Meghnad Desai or astronaut Sunita Williams, we believe that when Gujaratis do well abroad they always belong to Ahmedabad.

Many non-governmental organizations in the city are known to have links abroad, so speaking English has become important here along with languages like French, German, Dutch, Japanese and Mandarin, as goods with Made-in-China tags have flooded the market. Curiously, while families might object to the marriage of their wards with partners from other Indian religions or regions, they are more open to accepting spouses from America, England, Australia, France, Japan, Mexico or Kazakhstan, and prefer Western wear instead of traditional clothes. Saris draped in Gujarati style are worn only by women of some communities, older matrons or by young women during festivals like Navratri or weddings.

Women of most communities revere the alcove dedicated to Goddess Laxmi at Three Gates, better known as Teen Darwaza, inside the walled city of Ahmedabad. A straight road from here leads to the main entrance of the old city at Bhadra Fort, where Laxmi's right hand is carved on the right-hand-side doorway and worshipped. The goddess appears to be tall with small hands. The carving is at the entrance, which shows that she was standing at the main gate, inside the city, and the doors were closed behind her, so she could not leave the city.

Ahmedabad has gates, but no walls, yet the gates create illusionary walls around the city. I discovered the last wall of Ahmedabad with autorickshaw driver Mohammed Isaq. Imagine, being on the busy Nehru Bridge with Isaq driving his vehicle one-handed at full speed, while the other hand pointed

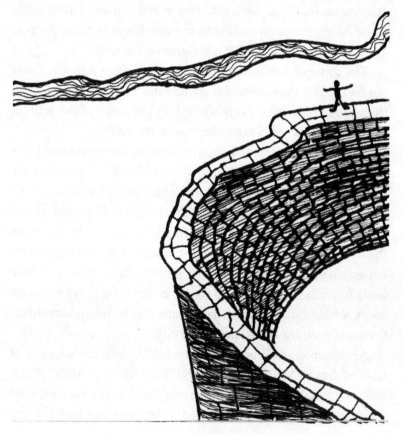

towards the last wall of Ahmedabad. He sat with one leg folded on his seat and seeing my anxious face in the rear-view mirror, he reassured me, saying, 'Nothing to worry.' Soon, he was giving a running commentary on the fortress. As a child he had played on the wall with his friends, running on its parapet from Cama Hotel to Shahpur's Shankar Bhuvan slums. It looks impossible because today, the wall stands shoulder to shoulder with apartment buildings of all shapes and sizes. Isaq knew the area like the back of his hand and took me whizzing past high-rise apartment buildings and interconnected narrow lanes, while showing me the steps leading to the watchtowers of the fortress at various points and other highlights of the wall.

The distance between the Pol houses and the wall was about ten feet, but if the new buildings had not been built so close to the wall, I could have easily walked on the ledge of the wall till the end, from where I could have seen the river.

A straight road from Shahpur's Shankar Bhuvan slums leads to Delhi Gate and Mahadevpura. Much before block print textiles became fashionable, they were available here. The place gets its name from a Mahadev temple built under an old peepal tree. It is also known as shoe market or mojdi bazaar, as this is where the intricately embroidered, hand-crafted traditional shoes with curled toes or mojdis are made by Rajasthani artisans. This lane leads towards Delhi Darwaza where chilli powder, dry turmeric roots, whole cumin and coriander are sold to prove that this is the most fragrant spice lane of the city.

Ahmedabad abounds in city stories. A well-known story is that of Manecknath, a sage who lived on the bank of the Sabarmati making quilts and weaving mats. For some reason he had a dispute with Sultan Ahmed Shah, who was building the fortress around the city. But, during the construction, walls built during the day turned to rubble at midnight, much to Ahmed Shah's bewilderment. He was mystified by the occurrence, till one of his informers told him that the fortress fell only when the saint pulled out the threads from the quilt he was making. The sultan decided to meet Manecknath. After innumerable discussions and agreeing to conditions set by the saint, the dispute was resolved and the fortress was built.

Another version of the same story is that the sultan challenged the saint to show his magical power by entering a bottle. When the saint agreed, the sultan trapped him by closing the lid, so that Manecknath was sealed inside the bottle and could not create obstructions in the building of Ahmedabad. Yet, there appears to be a twist in this story as, it is hard to believe that a man like Manecknath with his magical powers agreed to enter the bottle. If a thread from his quilt could bring down the walled city, how could he be tricked into entering a bottle?

It is said, Manecknath had a hypnotic presence with fiery green eyes set in a strong-boned face, a golden mane of hair, diamond studs in his ears and always wore a red silk robe. Maneck Chowk is the venue of Manecknath's samadhi. It is crammed between jewellery shops near Badshah No Hajiro and the queen's mosque, Rani No Hajiro.

Manecknath's shrine resembles a jewellery shop with a temple of Goddess Bahucharaji, a Shivalinga and an idol of Lord Ganesha, where rituals are performed at regular hours. It is near the Ahmedabad Stock Exchange and the first Pol of Ahmedabad—aptly known as Mahurat Ni Pol, as Mahurat means an auspicious new beginning. Here, there is an interesting wall, which is the back of a shop and covered with posters of gods and goddesses.

Over the last thirty years, the piping hot tea served at this stall, known as Maneckbhai's kitli, has become well known. An image of Lord Shiva is pasted in the centre of the wall, while images of other gods and goddesses cover the rest of the wall. Among the deities are Laxmi, Saraswati, Momai Mata, Kali, Meldi Mata, Dasha Maa, Hadkai Mata, Shitla Mata, Durga, Mahashakti, Khodiyar Mata, Ashapuri Mataji, Hanuman, Krishna, Sai Baba, Shankar and Parvati with Ganesha, while Sitaram Bapa is shown sitting cross-legged and drinking a cup of tea. On demand, Maneckbhai makes tea with less sugar and serves it in a cup. Tea parcels in polythene bags with plastic cups are also sent to shopkeepers and tea leaves are collected in a bucket to be given away as manure.

As Maneckbhai, owner of the kitli, made tea for me, I complimented him on the collage and asked what had prompted him to make it. Without looking up, he answered in just one word 'Bhakti'—faith.

This area is also known for mukhvas or mouth-freshening saunf or mints. A friend from Mumbai always asks for mukhvas from here. Before you reach this area, the fragrance from these shops hits you. These vendors are known as the mukhvas kings of Maneck Chowk. I have been their regular customer for years. The owner sits at the counter making the bill as employees cajole buyers to taste different varieties of mukhvas. Like French wine tasters, they play the role of official mukhvas tasters as they know the intricacies of each flavour and also know the choice of the regular buyers and start packing it as soon as they see one of them in the crowd. Next to these shops, there is an alcove in the wall with a stone idol of Lord Hanuman known as Jayshree Rokadnath dada. The owner explains, 'Rokadnath dada

is Hanuman's second name, because everything in this street is by rokdi, meaning: by cash, no udhar, no credit, pay now, not later.'

The shrine is made with white tiles. Hanuman is carved in rock and covered with silver leaf, inlaid with eyes of shell, and has a silver crown, as he stands under a silver umbrella against a painting of Ram and Sita, surrounded by images of Hanuman as a child sitting in his mother Anjani's lap, and strangely resembles a film star of the 1950s. This entire area is fragrant with mints

like rajbhog, lilo, moglai, bhameda and paanchur. The mukhvas kings also specialize in dried fruit, aamras papad, pickled figs like kharek and silver-coated cardamom.

At night, Maneck Chowk transforms into a food court, where Gujarati snacks are served along with unusual combinations like chocolate pizza, chilli ice cream and club sandwiches made with slices of fresh pineapple, grated cheese and jam. It is no longer easy to reach Maneck Chowk from Teen Darwaza, as the entire area around Bhadra Kali temple has been redesigned as a plaza for pedestrians. Earlier, a straight road from Bhadra Kali temple was the main artery to the walled city, where an elephant stood swaying its trunk amidst vendors selling coconut, incense sticks, lotus flowers, jackfruit, palm fruit, watermelon, musk melon, roasted mango seeds and ripe tamarind.

In the past, there were many more bakeries in the old city, where a loaf of bread is still known as dubble-roti, literally meaning a double-flatbread. Closer to Bhadra Fort, Italian Bakery is more organized and has Ahmedabad Ni Biscuit, a small, double-baked, stone-hard loaf of bread, which softens only when soaked in a cup of tea. In suburban Juhapura, Famous Bakery is situated on the way to Sarkhej Roza and has a wide range of biscuits, like naankhatai, coconut macaroon, biscuits with sesame seeds, coin-size wine biscuits, Danish rolls with jam, cream rolls and cupcakes, while Aflatoon with its golden glaze has been around since the existence of the city. The owners of these bakeries are sure that some of these recipes are as old as the darwazas or influenced by recipes made during the British Raj, as some biscuit moulds resemble floral motifs seen in mosques and one can still find black currant cake at some bakeries. Past Teen Darwaza, there is Huseini Bakery at Biscuit

Gully, which is known for naan or oven-baked, plate-sized roundels of white bread, pastry puffs with vegetable or chicken fillings and packets of salty, flaky khari biscuits. This road leads to Maneck Chowk vegetable market, where there is as much happening inside as outside. During summer, mango reigns supreme with poetic names like hafooz or Alphonso, kesar, badam, gulab, totapuri, neelam and sundari. This is where one finds mounds of green, raw Rajapuri, Vanraj and desi mangoes for pickling. The vendors oblige buyers by grating, cubing and asking, 'Do you have good pickle hands? If not, your pickle will develop fungus. To make a good pickle, you need good pickle hands.' Mangoes conjure images of eating the fruit in a hundred and one ways, cut, uncut, chewed, sucked, peeled, unpeeled, sliced, cubed and seductively slurped, as the juice trickles down the chin. In most homes, fresh mango juice is served with puffed wheat-flour puris and steamed dhokla, which is known as the perfect Gujarati lunch. Amusingly, a soup-like kadhi known as fajeto, which means scandal, is also made with mango leftovers to prove that the women of the house had made full use of the fruit. Raw mangoes are used to make baflo or panna, a salty sweet-sour drink to ward off heat stroke during the fierce summer, along with chutneys, pickles and a salad of grated raw mango, onions, chillies and jaggery.

Maneck Chowk is also known for phalsa berries, figs, raw tamarind, chikoo, corn on the cob, papaya, gooseberries, bananas, sugar cane juice, limbu paani, watermelon, pineapple, lassi, faluda, matka kulfi, crushed ice-slush gola and much more, as Hanuman looks down at the diverse fare and smiles.

The old city has many narrow lanes like old Phool Gully or flower market near Dhalgarwad, which became known for its traffic jams, so that eventually it was shifted to Jamalpur, opposite the last chimney of Calico Mill. It is a fascinating place and retains the energy of the original flower bazaar. Then, it was situated near Badshah No Hajiro, where there was a naubatkhana for the royal drummers, situated atop the entrance of the mausoleum, from where drums were played during the reign of Sultan Ahmed Shah.

A path leads into Jama Masjid, built in 1424. It is an impressive monument in sandstone with a waterbody, a colonnade on three sides, and quiet interiors. The grave of the sultan's trusted chowkidar, Chobdar Baba, is next to the gate. As a tradition, some security guards still worship the chowkidars of such ancient religious sites, so that nothing untoward happens at their workplace. Drums are still played here late in the evening as a form of loyalty to the sultan by the ancestors of his chief drummer. The waqf committee pays them a salary, as they are custodians of the naubatkhana.

Rani No Hajiro, opposite Badshah No Hajiro, is the main hub of activity in the old city with its textile and jewellery shops. Tazias are also made here during Muharram. The queens from Sultan Ahmed Shah's royal family are buried here.

The character of the city keeps changing, but never its essence. This has been retained, even when efforts were made to change the city's name from Ahmedabad to Karnavati after Karnadeva Solanki, who ruled over this region around AD 1074. Ahmedabad has a mixed bag of stories and one of them is a ghost story set around the mosque of Hazrat Ashiq Ali Bava near Usmanpura crossroads, situated behind a municipal garden lined with trees, with a ragged lawn, pathways for joggers, benches for senior citizens and a pavilion covered with bougainvillea ablaze with bright magenta flowers. Behind this pretty picture, there is a small gate which leads to the mosque, where there are three graves, covered with flowers and oil lamps. Every Thursday evening, the caretaker of the mosque is known to cure the possessed, and devotees from all communities believe in him. At the entrance of the mosque, they dip their fingers into the warm oil of clay lamps burning there and rub it on their bodies, as it is believed that rubbing oil and eating the petals of the red roses strewn on the grave cures mentally ill people. The place swarms with hundreds of people, waiting in silence, screaming or shouting, as a woman with long, black hair swirls like a dancing dervish in the centre of the courtyard.

We also have sites dedicated to a walking saint, coughing saint, laughing saint and talking saint, sort of a speech therapist who taught children to speak correctly. His dargah caters to problems connected with the mouth, tongue, gums and teeth which are resolved by licking the sugar spread on the steps of the mosque. After which, the devotees drink water from a water chute, which has an amazing story. When the saint went on Haj, he forgot his ritualistic vessel there. On return, he banged his hands in despair on the ground and a spring sprouted from that very place. A popular belief amongst devotees is that the spring is connected with the waters of Zamzam in Mecca.

In a similar vein, there is a story that the Bhadra Fort had a tunnel leading to Vadodara, which is well over a hundred kilometres away. Built around Azam Khan's palace, it has huge gateways large enough for elephants to pass through, and a staircase leading to a clocktower.

On the busy Tilak Road, near Bhadra Fort and Teen Darwaza,

there is the quaint shrine known as Hasti Bibi No Gokhlo, a small marble niche on the back wall of a tailor's shop. Her name is written in Gujarati and it has a donation box, below the alcove, which is at eye level, so that a child sitting on its mother's arm can easily look into the shrine. According to legend, about five hundred years ago, Hasti Bibi lived in Ahmedabad and had the power to heal a child by holding it in her arms and making it laugh. This belief continues; so lamps are lit, donations given and jalebis offered to Hasti Bibi.

In Ahmedabad, if we have shaking minarets, we also have a dargah which walks, making it into a magical city. This small nondescript dargah near Dariapur crossroads houses the grave of Hazrat Gulam Mohmed Saiyyed, the Walking Saint of Ahmedabad. Hundreds of threads are tied by devotees on the grills. It is believed that every year, the dargah moves, inching towards the centre of the road. They say the saint listens to pleas of the needy and bestows boons on them. When a wish is granted, a metal lock is attached to the grill, so that the problem is locked away forever. The same magical quality can be experienced at the mysterious Shaking Minarets of Ahmedabad, better known as Jhulta Minaras or the Mosque of Siddi Bashir,

in the Sarangpur area. Ahmedabad has two sets of shaking minarets. The pious feel that the spiritual power of Siddi Bashir makes the minarets shake, while others say they were built to counter earthquakes.

It is generally believed that the engineering secrets of the minarets died with the craftsmen who built them. Before the minarets were closed down for visitors, some fifty years back, one could still climb the enormous steps spiralling upwards.

Ahmedabad is also known for the Siddi Saiyyed mosque and its intricately carved windows depicting The Tree of Life, which is often used as a logo by most institutions of the city. Set like an oasis in a maze of traffic, it has a waterbody, foliage and trees, which merge with the stone tracery, complete with floral and geometric forms surrounded by delicately carved creepers and palm trees.

Ahmedabad has a small African community, known as Siddis. They came to India from East Africa as slaves during the eleventh century with Arab and Portuguese traders. Jhujhar Khan ruled over Ahmedabad for a short period, but when Emperor Akbar conquered Ahmedabad, he refused to surrender, and was eventually captured and crushed to death by a royal elephant and buried at Sarkhej Roza. Siddiwada at Patharkuva on Tilak Road is the stronghold of this community. They are Muslims, but they follow some Hindu rituals and have made a name for themselves with their traditional trance-like dance known as Siddi Dhamaal in India and across the world, where they are invited to give performances.

It is generally believed that the old city of Ahmedabad does not have enough green cover. This is not true as most mosques have trees and a waterbody, like Rani Roopvati's mosque at Mirzapur near a famous samosa shop.

Bhatiyar Gully is nearby, at the entrance of Teen Darwaza. Since the last six hundred years, this lane is known for its master chefs.

They make the best mutton samosas, like the ones made at a small stall in Mirzapur, which are special, different and addictive. Similar samosas are also available at Kalupur, Jamalpur and Juhapura.

Maybe, samosas of one shop may be spicier than those from another, but generally they retain a certain standard taste. Fried, crusty and brown, the taste of mince along with chopped onions laced with a dash of green chilli and garlic with the fat oozing ever so lightly—eating them is an unforgettable experience.

As the swifts swirl over Teen Darwaza, the entire area exudes the flavours of Arabia with kebabs, samosas, fried fish, mincemeat, bheja fry, tandoori chicken, curries of chicken and mutton, and biryani cooking in large blackened vessels which sit on iron coal stoves, next to the Bara Haandis or twelve varieties of meat dishes simmering over a slow fire, so that clients can choose and order accordingly.

They also have oven-baked, round, plate-sized white yeast bread made in a salty-sweet dough, plain or layered with nuts, with mincemeat filling or baked with eggs atop and known as naan or khummas.

Here, biryani is made with Basmati rice, chana dal, meat, whole potatoes and boiled eggs, fragrant with saffron, spiced with garam masala and sprinkled with golden brown petals of deep-fried onion, birasta. Many Ahmedabadis still prefer to buy meat, chicken, fish, shrimps and eggs at Bhatiyar Gully. They have their regulars from where they have been buying for years,

ESTHER DAVID

and even if they live in west Ahmedabad, they go shopping early in the morning to avoid the traffic. It is not a place for the weak-hearted, as there is a mixed fragrance of cooked and uncooked flesh, and stray dogs stalk the streets along with crows and kites, which swoop down to snatch pieces of meat. It has workshops and residences of Muslim chefs known as bhatiyaras or bawarchis, who only take large orders for weddings, festivals and parties. Their kitchens resemble open garages with coal stoves, enormous vessels and large griddles to make napkin-size chapattis, known as mandas, which can be eaten with curries or used to wrap samosas. Known for their culinary artistry, they have joined hands with tour operators and fly to Dubai or make food for Haj pilgrims, carrying their vessels and condiments with them. There is also a variant known as Chinese-Mughlai food, which is made at Kalupur tower. To watch these cooks is a delightful experience. It is like a game, as their hands move like acrobats who never miss a movement—in their case, ingredient. It is a skill which comes from long practice of quickly mixing different condiments without burning the food and serving it without wasting a minute and moving on to the next order. With the ladle flying in the air, these swashbuckling chefs can make thirty varieties of Chinese-Mughlai, like Schezwan, Hakka, Hong Kong, Singaporean and Manchurian.

If the old city of Ahmedabad has bakeries, we have a bread-wallah in our area. It is not a profession that a young man like Nayumuddin would choose on his own, as most teenagers of his age work as peons, courier boys, electricians, plumbers or pizza delivery boys. But Nayumuddin decided to continue with his family business of selling bakery products, which are kept in a box strapped to his cycle. He is a good-looking youth with sharp features and big, dreamy eyes. He likes to wear a sports cap, jeans, T-shirt and sneakers bought from the Sunday Market. Late afternoon, he goes from society to society, house to house selling bread and biscuits. He likes to stop and talk to me about trees, as he reminisces about the bamboo clump behind his family house in a village near Ghaziabad, but he likes Ahmedabad and lives in a rented room in Jamalpur. His day starts by filling water, cooking, washing clothes, cleaning the house, checking his cycle, wiping the bread box and dressing for work. Every day, he collects his quota of bread and biscuits from wholesalers and starts work around noon, cycling down on his regular route, calling out in a loud voice, B-R-E-A-D, so that we know that he has arrived. Sometimes, he visits an aunt who invites him for dinner, but he prefers to be self-sufficient and likes to attend communal festivities, fairs, weddings or an Urs.

For me, Eid also means meeting Faiz Mohmed, an old family friend, who still lives near our ancestral house at Delhi Gate. Even after we moved from there, he always comes to meet us. He arrives in an autorickshaw, his hair freshly hennaed, dressed in a crisp white Pathani dress, embroidered vest, mojdis, giving off a whiff of ittar and carrying a tiffin carrier full of biryani. He is older, sits on the edge of the chair with a glass of rose sherbet in hand, remembering the good old days, and leaves hurriedly with a wistful salaam.

During Ramzan, the scene at Bhatiyar Gully is different. This is when the homeless, poor and hungry sit in rows on the footpath. The hoardings on these shops explain the rules for feeding Bapus, a dignified term used for beggars. They sit there awaiting donors, who visit these eateries and give money to feed the hungry. Stacks of tandoori rotis are made as vessels of steaming hot food are kept ready with vegetable curry, dal, rice and chicken curry. Normally, for a minimum donation of ten to fifteen rupees, the owner serves a vegetarian platter. But, if a Bapu asks for chicken curry, the owner serves it without complaint. It is said that no one leaves this place hungry, as there is a constant stream of donors. This process continues from midday to midnight. These are small canteens, which have tables and benches for Bapus and regular customers. Women in this group are given food packets as it is not considered safe for them to sit with the men.

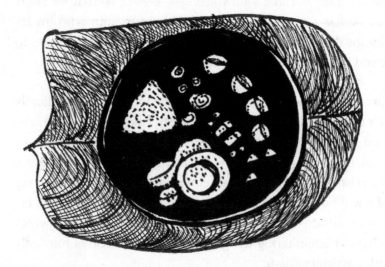

From Teen Darwaza, Gandhi Road leads towards Fernandez Bridge and Chandravilas, one of the first thali restaurants of Ahmedabad, which used to sell a thali for one rupee once. They were also famous for sixteen varieties of tea, like bagicha, amiri and gulabi, etc., which could be had for twenty-five paise at one time. Chandravilas was known as a lodge or dining hall. Old-timers remember that even before you reached it, the fragrance of their famous sour-sweet dal hit you. It was a secret recipe made with thirty-eight ingredients and after you had eaten there, the flavour lingered on the fingertips for hours. Some food lovers went there just for the dal or took it back home in containers.

Chandravilas is still famous for its deep-fried, flute-shaped fafdas made with chickpea dough along with jalebis, fried in ghee and soaking in sugar syrup, which is a favourite combination with Ahmedabadis. It is still popular with people looking for the best and are willing to travel that extra kilometre to get it. Chandravilas was started by Chimanlal Joshi, whose grandson Malay sits at the same counter where his father sat doing brisk business. Chimanlal had advised his family, 'Always make jalebis in ghee and you will survive for more than a hundred years,' and they did. Before the Chandravilas thali closed down, Ahmedabadis went to Rani No Hajiro for their wedding shopping and stopped at Chandravilas for a meal. It was like a pilgrimage of sorts. As a rule, most Gujaratis did not like to eat with their shoes on, so a special place was allotted to wash their feet and keep their shoes far away from the dining area. Well-known names patronized Chandravilas—Malay points to a table which was Indulal Yagnik's favourite place, and whenever film star Raj Kapoor was in Ahmedabad, his host, a theatre owner, ordered food from Chandravilas. It was an exclusive eatery, as the dining room had oak chairs from France and the ceiling fans with wood fittings were assembled by a British carpenter. This thali was incomplete without steamed khaman-khandvi made in a chickpea batter, lentil-based dahivadas, jacket potatoes in gravy, vegetables, paper-thin chapattis, puffed puris, buttermilk, onion rings, green chillies, a sliver of lemon, papad, dal and rice served with a dollop of ghee, along with jalebis. Special thalis, minus some ingredients, like onions, garlic and potatoes, were available for Jain clients, but washing hands in the thali was prohibited; instead a bowl was placed under the table or they washed hands at the copper basin, which is still part of their legacy.

When you are in a hurry, a thali in Ahmedabad can be served in less than five minutes and still be a satisfying meal. A thali can be best described as a twelve-inch platter of steel, brass, bell metal, copper or silver, with small bowls placed within to serve dal; a yogurt-based, soup-like kadhi; curry-based vegetables; and a sweet, syrupy gulab jamun or yogurt-based sweet shrikhand. Waiters serve hot chapattis, thinner puffed phulkas or deep-fried puris to accompany the variety of lightly spiced vegetables. A fried snack is a must, along with a salad of cucumber, stuffed green chillies, onion rings or garlic chutney for non-Jains, mango pickles, green chutney, slivers of lemon, papad and buttermilk. A bowl of aamras—mango juice—is served during summer, or a piece of sweet sukhadi made with wheat flour, jaggery and ghee. In winter, a millet flatbread is served with brinjals or undhiyu, a typical south Gujarat recipe made with almost all the vegetables mixed into it. Gujarati food has a spicy, sour-sweet flavour, as often, almost everything is sweetened, and largely criticized by non-Gujaratis for this trait. An unknown fact about Chandravilas is that along with the images of Goddess Laxmi and Lord Ganesha, they also have the shrine of a Turkish Sufi saint, which is covered with a shimmering green grave cover and roses, as an eternal light burns there for the last 125 years. Gujarati food symbolizes the 'Navras' or nine flavours of life, a concept which brings to it an incredible combination of rang-roop-swad—colour, appearance and taste. La Bella is also a popular eatery in Khanpur near Nehru Bridge. Close to the last wall in the old city, it is a simple place known for its non-vegetarian food, served with that extra ingredient called love. There is no signboard, just a dining area and kitchen. It is run by Aunty Mary, a little woman, who feeds homesick students from Ahmedabad's famous institutes since 1962, along with her dedicated helper Anna, alias Raju Pillai. She knows everything about these students and amuses them with stories about known names who were her clients, like film star Parveen Babi, who often had lunch at La Bella while studying at a college in Ahmedabad. Mary came to Ahmedabad from Anjuna, Goa, when she married Anthony John Lobo, and brought a touch of the Konkan coast to La Bella. Since her husband died, her canteen is often closed, due to financial problems and harassment from miscreants, who try to hound her out of Khanpur, but she holds on to her bastion with cudgel and knife and the help of some of her regulars. Home is a third-floor, two-room flat in a dialpidated building, where she sits on her tattered sofa watching cookery shows on television with vacant eyes. Till the early 1990s, except for members of Christian communities, Ahmedabadis never celebrated Christmas like other festivals. Suddenly in the mid-1990s, after the tremendous commercial success of St Valentine's Day, roses and greeting cards were sold at astronomical prices and the whole city was decorated with heart-shaped balloons. Cake shops were flooded with customers and restaurants were heavily booked in advance.

In December, Santa Claus masks are sold all over the city, along with plastic Christmas trees, Chinese paper lamps and red caps.

Shopkeepers hire unemployed men to dress as Santa and amuse children. A woman Santa visits old people's homes and a school for physically challenged children with a bag full of gifts, to keep alive the spirit of Christmas in the city.

Some celebrate festivals like Janmashtami at home in their ancestral bungalow-style havelis. It is the perfect setting to celebrate the festival, where an idol of baby Krishna is placed on a silver throne in the family temple or ghar-mandir inside the house, and the ringing of brass bells announces his birth at the stroke of midnight. Offerings include Lord Krishna's favourite ghee-soaked, syrupy, gram-flour mohanthal.

These havelis have high-ceilinged rooms, Persian carpets, old rosewood furniture with new upholstery, ancient clocks, chandeliers, antique stoneware jars, frilled lamps, wooden brackets, sacred painted textiles like Pichwais, terraces, balconies and a mosaic-tiled open courtyard surrounded by trees, where a family of peafowl roosts in the kadamb tree and calls on moonlit nights. Trees and worship are connected, like Shri Manavtavala Hanumanji temple built around a peepal tree, which gives it the name Peepaleshwar Mahadeva. This tree is strung with clusters of coconuts, near the overbridge at the IIM—Indian Institute of Management. It houses an idol of Hanuman in marble, along with Goddess Khodiyar, Peepaleshwar Mahadev, a Shivalinga, Nandi and Ganesha. During rush hour, it is impossible to stand near the temple and admire the massive peepal trunk shooting out of the temple roof, adorned with saffron flags. When a wish is fulfilled, garlands of coconut are tied to the tree and it is known as Shri Peepaleshwar Mahadeva.

One of this temple's devotees is Ramattar. He is often seen crossing the road from this temple to his tea stall on the pavement outside the IIM. Since 1982, he has been serving tea to students from a small aperture in the wall. Behind the wall, a cafe-like atmosphere has been created with benches and driftwood furniture. Ramattar sits on an empty packing case, from where he maintains a regular supply of tea, coffee, buns, omelettes, bidis and cigarettes. He is very popular with students, almost like Aunty Mary, and is part of IIM, as he is a little man with a big story. He lives in a small, two-room shanty in Vejalpur. The story of his life is similar to that of many migrant families who come to bigger cities looking for work. He belongs to Devapura, in Faizabad district of Uttar Pradesh, where his father was a farmer. But, when his mother died, he was sent to live with his elder brother, who worked as a gardener at Ahmedabad's Physical Research Laboratory, which is opposite the IIM. Ramattar is often featured in local newspapers as a success story. He is squat, energetic, has sharp eyes, sports a French beard with a lock of hair falling on his forehead, and is always dressed in trousers, shirts and a sports cap. Ramattar is easy-going, affectionate, ready to chat, often sharing his lunch with students, giving them a feeling of finding a home away from home. Many more teashops have cropped up all along the wall, but Ramattar is still very popular, and ex-students also keep in touch with him. Lately, every year in January, Ramattar takes a day off to see the international kite festival on the river front with family and friends.

The river front is also the venue for flower shows, water sports, speedboat rides, floating restaurants, gardens, promenades, food courts, marathons, beach sports, volleyball, football and cyclothons. Even if a cycle costs up to two lakh rupees or more, with extras for sports gear, accessories and shoes, Ahmedabadis are buying all these to keep up with the Joneses on the river front. Everything is available in Ahmedabad, whether it is designer helmets, tights, T-shirts, trainers or yoga-wear. Often, our cyclists look like they are competing in the Tour de France. Some young people create shock waves by dressing like Gujarati cowherds for these events, while bikers dress like actors from the Hindi film *Dhoom*. So what if the roads are bumpy and there are traffic jams galore. As a young enthusiast said, 'We no longer have to fly down to Singapore; we have it all here ...'

When I hear praises about the river front, I find myself thinking about rivers. So, while going to Vadodara, it was interesting to study the landscape between both cities. When the bus was on the Expressway, I saw a hoarding about New Maninagar and wondered whether they were going to chop down old trees to make high-rise apartment buildings or shopping complexes. It was a pleasure to see the expanse of green fields, dotted with women in colourful saris working in the fields, turbaned rabaris from the cowherd community riding motorbikes in their traditional dresses, canals, buffaloes soaking in shallow ponds and herds of cows walking past fenced fields. The post-monsoon sky changed colour as I spotted egrets, herons, dabchicks, drongos, shrikes and peafowl. The bus sped past Meshvo, Vatrak and Mahi rivers, seductively curving through mango groves and banana plantations, as I enjoyed the landscape.

According to folklore, when the city was being built, Sabarmati had almost changed course and was moving away from her present route, which cuts through the city. Baba Lalu'i (AD 1560), often pronounced as Baba Lablabi, who lived by the river, noticed this strange phenomenon; so he stood there with outstretched arms, beckoned the river back at his doorstep and asked her to flow through Ahmedabad. The saint belonged to the hallowed circle around Sultan Ahmed Shah, who was then making the blueprint of Ahmedabad. Eventually, Baba Lalu'i built a mosque on the bank of the river and is also buried there. This very elegant mosque is situated opposite the National Institute of Design near Sardar Patel Bridge; close by is the Flower Bazaar. Ahmedabad has always had a Sunday Market on the banks of the Sabarmati. It extends from Ellis Bridge to Gaekwad Ni Haveli, a long fortress which is a remnant of Maratha rule in Gujarat and built in 1753 by Damaji Gaekwad. The Marathas' combined army with Raghunath Rao Peshva brought an end to Mughal rule in Ahmedabad. This market came into being in 1414, when Sultan Ahmed Shah decided to have an open market known as Khaas Bazaar on Fridays, also known as Shukravari.

It was spread out from Teen Darwaza to Bhadra Fort, but through the years, its venue changed thrice. It is now held on Sundays, and known as Ravivari or Gujari Bazaar, near the river and around the fortress of Maneck Burj at Ellis Bridge in east Ahmedabad. This market is spread on the broad pavements of the river front, along a path lined with trees, temples and shrines. From early morning to late evening, it is jampacked from Khamasa Circle to Bal Gangadhar Tilak Municipal Garden, also known as Victoria Garden, to Gaekwad Ni Haveli. Old timers remember that they could buy antiques, chandeliers, furniture, utensils, brassware and goats at this market. Caged monitor lizards were also available as their organs were known to work as potent aphrodisiacs. Just about everything is available here for the asking at unimaginable prices, like recycled saris and shirts for ten, twenty or a hundred rupees. Ladders can be bought at reasonable prices, along with coffee tables, mirrors, T-shirts, sports shoes, jeans, chairs, dog chains, swing chains, charpoy strings, handbags with fake designer tags, cheap perfume, plastic toys, kidswear, ribbons, hair clips, bangles, handkerchiefs, vessel stands, iron scrap, nutcrackers, locks shaped like animals, posters of gods . . . even out-of-print books and old coins. Announcements are made on loudspeakers, as vendors sell water pouches, paani-puris—crisp fried puris, filled with tangy water—potatoes with lentils, chilled pineapple slices and fresh lime juice.

An entire area is allotted to rat traps to counter the city's vermin population. This department is a designer's delight with traps in all sizes, so much so, that you start wondering about the size of the rats which live in Ahmedabad. The highlight of this area is the chuhe-maarnewallah chacha or rat catcher. He looks like a knight from the Middle Ages as he wears a life-size placard, which covers him and is painted with every possible creepy, crawly creature which abounds in Ahmedabad, from mice, rats, lizards, bugs, mosquitoes to cockroaches. He ensures the elimination of these pests with his poison potions, which he carries in a shoulder bag. Death, he says, is instant. There is a sense of foreboding as he sells his ware and a robot installed amidst antiques predicts the future of the city.

Ahmedabad has two Pols which are named after goats. Bakra Pol is inhabited by Hindus and Bakri Pol by Muslims, where almost every family owns goats marked with henna designs to identify their owners. Bakra Pol, near Dariapur chakla on the way to Chalte Pir Ki Dargah, is a quaint little area which has tall

and narrow three-storeyed houses with tiled roofs, carved wooden brackets and fluted pillars, painted in yellow and blue. The doors are painted in bright green, and colourful quilts are spread out on string cots. All along the footpath, near the bus stand, the residents of Bakra Pol sell parakeets, rabbits and budgerigars, as their owners make birdcages. This Pol belongs to the Devi Pujak community known to be artisans, as they paint on sacred textiles known as Mata Ni Pachedi. During certain rituals, a witch doctor invokes the goddess at midnight, while narrating a story set against the backdrop of the cloth, and sacrifices a black goat as a tantric ritual. Sometimes, it is used as a temporary place of worship in the absence of a temple. These craftspeople work on textiles with block prints, and paint in the ancient Kalamkari technique with red and black vegetable dyes. Devi Pujaks are short, sturdy, have a beautiful copper colour, and can nimbly traverse the length and breadth of the city by autorickshaws or hopping on and off buses or just walking.

A road from here leads to Relief Road. It reaches a small street near Fernandez Bridge, Patasa Ni Pol and Suhagan Centre which belongs to three generations of the Kanchwallah family, well known for their expertise at piercing ears. This family has been practising the art for a hundred years and is also known as Ghughrawallah, as a brass bell hangs from the ceiling which they ring to distract the attention of a crying child while the ears are being pierced.

Nafisa, Tasneem and their father take turns at piercing ears. As I watch, they pinpoint the place on a young girl's ear or nose with a ballpen, apply spirit and quickly pierce it with a silver or gold ring, as a child's delicate skin might react to cheap alloys and become septic. Gently, a piece of wire is knotted with pliers

and a mirror is held up, so that the customer can see their handiwork. They also pierce eyebrows, tongues, lower chin and belly buttons, which are done at their residence in Kalupur. They are also adept at the gunshot method, with which they shoot a silver ring into the earlobe with a specially devised staple gun. The Kanchwallahs have also learned acupuncture to cure migraine and backache, so it is much more than just piercing ears that they do.

Fernandez Bridge is a fun bridge; it is neither street nor lane, but a mini-bridge. Maybe, it is Ahmedabad's first flyover-cum-underbridge, which is actually a part of Gandhi Road, and walking under the bridge or above it is an exciting experience.

One has to literally jostle through the crowd to reach

Fernandez Bridge, as the area under the bridge, also known as Kagdiwaad, is a haven for merchants selling reams of paper, handcrafted account books, notebooks and textbooks, both new and second-hand. Greeting cards or wedding cards are also available at nominal rates. It is a wholesaler's paradise, as vendors sit in their shops or outside on the broken steps of the bridge selling their ware along with wooden prayer beads, rudraksha and cowrie shells.

Below this bridge, there is Lokhand Bazaar, which immediately conjures images of iron and steel. Instead, this is a colourful place, with rows of shops selling silk threads, garlands for gods, brocade turbans for a bridegrooms, black thread to tie to the talisman of a newborn baby, accessories for Hindu weddings and the like. This lane also hits Chandla Pol, where silversmiths repair broken jewellery in a matter of minutes.

Next door, Vali Mohamed has one of the smallest shops in

Ahmedabad. He is a famous rafoo master, well known for his skill at darning. Sure, there are many laundries where clothes are darned, but often they refuse if the fabric is frayed. His shop is a four-by-two space crammed between larger shops, where he stores bundles of saris, dupattas, shawls, a variety of threads and boxes of beads and sequins. He works with his sons and is known to be an expert at repairing old Banarsi saris. Valibhai learnt the art of darning old clothes from his mother and now his sons have followed in his footsteps. This is one of those amazing stories of Ahmedabad, where one can still find master craftspeople in the many nooks and corners of the city.

Doshiwada Ni Pol is close to Lokhand Bazaar and the most unlikely place to find peace, amidst innumerable shops of sandalwood, incense, ittar or perfume made from flowers, camphor, saffron and snack shops, known for their spicy banana chips.

The Jain Vidyashala Trust is a sales centre for Jain sadhus and nuns, housed in an old building. Its cool dark interiors exude subdued fragrances of sandalwood and saffron. Salespersons at the Vidyashala explain patiently that the fly whisk is made with wool; dandasan is a long walking stick and patra sets made in turned wood are an assortment of vessels, dishes, bowls, plates, pots and glasses of all sizes used by Jain ascetics and can be stacked together. Special shawls and blankets are sold here for sadhus.

The Jain community of Ahmedabad has contributed in a big way to the economy of the city. A lavish ceremony is held with a procession of elephants and camels and a horse carriage in which the monk-to-be is seated when one of them decides to renounce the worldly life.

The legendary Shantidas Zaveri was a wealthy Jain jeweller of Ahmedabad and held in respect by Emperor Akbar. Shantidas had hosted Empress Jodhabai's stay in Ahmedabad and was conferred with the title of 'Nagarseth', meaning, an eminent citizen of the city. Later, Harkunvar Sethani, widow of Seth Hutheesing, completed the construction of a Jain temple, which is known to be a fine example of its kind in the city.

In Ahmedabad, most people wear talismans, which are available in every possible nook and corner of the old city. These are also available at Lokhand Bazaar or at a small stall near Jamalpur Circle, where they have some unusual silver-plated talismans, grave coverings and bedis or copper-wire anklets. They also keep smaller talismans embossed with shapes of eyes, ears, tongue, brain, head, body, lungs, heart, hands, legs, intestines, the palm of a hand, houses, autorickshaws, trucks, cars, horses and vehicles. When a wish is fulfilled, one of these talismans is offered at the dargah as a form of thanksgiving.

Suburban Ahmedabad always had a resident potter, who worked on a hand wheel, sitting hunched under a banyan tree, and like a magician created innumerable pots from just one ball of clay. I still remember the potter in Vastrapur gaam, who made small handle-less disposable cups or kulhars to serve water, tea or lassi. He also made terracotta water pots or matkas for the home, clay lamps or diyas, and other ritualistic articles for festivals, along with idols of gods and pot-bellied piggy banks. When the water pots were made, they were dried on the roof of the potter's house. When dry, they were painted with a wash of earth colours like red ochre by the women of the potter's family and arranged in an earthen kiln, covered with fodder, rice husk, wood shavings and dry cow dung cakes. After the earthenware was fired, the pots were cooled and cleaned, and the potter made sure that they were waterproof by playing a beat on each pot, checking it for cracks. So, whenever a potter passes by with water pots stacked on a four wheeler, I am saddened by the fact that they are no longer part of our daily life. Yet, it is heartening that most religious sites of the city have a parab or water place, an ancient Gujarati tradition of offering water to people passing by a religious place or even a tree.

Gheekanta, in the old city, is a stronghold of Saraniyas, an artisan community which sharpens knives, scissors and swords. This is where ghee was weighed and sold in huge containers. But, since Ahmedabadis became health conscious and reduced the intake of ghee, these shops closed down. Similarly, Shah-e-Alam is known for its scissor-sharpening shops and became a second home for Saraniyas. So when people of west Ahmedabad do not want to go to the walled city to sharpen a knife or repair a pair of scissors, they wait for the monthly visit of a Saraniya. On Sunday mornings, they arrive on a bicycle with various sharpening gadgets attached to the front basket and back seat.

Saraniyas employ two methods to sharpen knives. Sometimes, they carry a wooden stand, which has a wheel and cannot be carried on the shoulder, so they hire an autorickshaw or cycle rickshaw to transport it. Recently, they have taken to bicycles, which are specially altered to carry their ware.

The bicycle is an all-in-one shop, as next to the seat, there is a pulley with an emery stone fixed to the handle, attached to a leather strap tied to the wheel. The Saraniya pedals on his stationary vehicle and sharpens knives on the emery. A plastic spoon holder is attached to the handlebar, decorated with deadly looking knives, while the back seat has a toolbox.

Saraniyas have an interesting dress code, which suits their craft. They wear colourful T-shirts over loose trousers, either with a beret or a bandana. They look dangerous and people hesitate to get their knives sharpened by them, but there is no need to worry, as they are willing to chat and give a detailed narrative on the art of sharpening knives and swords. They are often invited by temples and ex-royals living in the city or even people who own swords and need to sharpen and polish their weapons.

Artisans who make brooms also live around Shah-e-Alam. Earlier, brooms were made in all sizes by artisans, who lived alongwith Saraniyas and carpenters who made cricket bats for children, which were also used by women to wash clothes.

Like sharpening knives, making jhadoos or brooms is also an art. I often see a family making brooms in the compound of an empty bungalow in Ambawadi. I noticed how after making the brooms, they checked their girth, length and weight by shaking them in the air or beating them on the floor.

In Gujarati, the word for broom is savarni, which has a feminine sound and is used to sweep the floor, while savarna, which sounds masculine, is made with dry reeds and used to wash bathrooms. Such shorter brooms are also used to sweep clay-plastered floors and the longer ones with short, V-shaped, hard stalks are used to sweep gardens. Smaller, softer reeds are tied to long handles, as they help clean ceilings. In recent times, brooms are made in plastic with an adjustable handle, along with brooms for bathrooms, which are made with colourful plastic stalks.

For the last few years, these artisans are no longer seen on pavements. Instead, dealers and middlemen have standardized the design of jhadoos for supermarkets.

Ahmedabad has many green zones, like Gandhi Ashram, also known as Satyagraha Ashram or Sabarmati Ashram, situated on the river front. The ashram has many trees, and whenever I am there, I cannot help but think of them as Mahatma Gandhi's trees. I touch the bark of the tree near Hriday Kunj, the cottage which was his residence, and feel blessed.

Tourists from abroad often take a small piece of bark from the neem tree here as a memento. At the entrance, a map indicates that a tamarind tree, which fell in 1972, had witnessed all the events of the ashram, established by Gandhiji on 17 June 1917. He had moved from Kochrab near Paldi bus stand and chosen the Sabarmati river bed as the ideal location for the ashram. The map also mentions a ghat leading to the river, a cowshed or Gaushala, and Saint Dadhichi's samadhi. Near Gandhi Ashram, a tree-lined lane leads to the lesser-known Doodhadhari Mahadeva and Dadhichi Rishi Nu Ashram. It is belived that when large quantities of milk are poured on the Shivalinga by ardent devotees, the milk flows into the river. Amidst these dilapitaded houses, under an old banyan tree, there is a temple dedicated to Shri Maharshi Dadhichi Rishi, where a small seated idol of the bearded saint is housed in a glass diorama, along with a life-size painting, in the community prayer hall. There are smaller shrines of Lord Bhairavnath, Shri Aghori Dada and Bhala Bapa Kana Bapa, venerated by the cowherd Bharwad community, as they celebrate Lord Krishna's birth or Janmashtami with a mini-fair and the traditional garba dance. An interesting feature of this place is that devotees offer prayers to all the temples and make offerings of cigarettes to Shri Aghori Dada as a form of wish-fulfilment. According to Hindu mythology, Dadhichi had hidden the weapons of the gods in his spine and renounced his body when they wanted them back to fight an army of demons.

Gandhi Ashram is now a tourist site with a museum, which traces the pictorial history of the freedom struggle. There is a library and sales counter where books cost anything from one rupee to five hundred, along with mini charkhas, CDs of Mahatma Gandhi's favourite bhajans and books of Gandhi Katha by Narayan Desai, son of Gandhiji's personal assistant Mahadev Desai.

In Hriday Kunj, Gandhiji's belongings are on display with his favourite figurines of three monkeys, which signify 'see no evil, speak no evil and hear no evil'. A larger version of the same can be seen on the lawns with a bronze statue of the Mahatma seated cross-legged in meditation near Upasana Mandir, where he held prayer meetings under the trees.

The ashram is almost always full of visitors, especially on Sundays, when one can see people from all over India and abroad walking on the grounds with reverence. Locals with their children are also seen here with picnic baskets and cameras.

The museum has some interesting quotes by the Mahatma, like this one: 'I am mostly busy making sandals. I have already made about 15 pairs. When you need new ones, please send me the measurements. And, when you do so, mark the places where the strap has to be fixed, that is on the outer side of the big toe and the little one.'

At Gandhi Ashram, I walk around the museum or just sit on the steps leading to the river and watch the birds roosting in the trees.

Ashram Road is named aptly, as it starts from Gandhiji's old ashram at Kochrab and goes onwards to Gujarat Vidyapeeth, the university started by him, along with Navjeevan Press, past Usmanpura crossroads, at Vadaj, which has a settlement of wood carvers and patchwork artisans. Ashram Road ends at Gandhi Ashram near Sabarmati Jail.

In 1930, when Gandhiji started the Salt March, he had vowed that he would not return to the ashram unless he gained freedom for India from the British Raj. He never returned. Exactly as he had said, 'If blood be shed, let it be our own. Let us cultivate the calm courage to die without killing.'

It was Mahatma Gandhi's vision to make eco-friendly indigenous products, especially khadi and handmade paper known as kalamkhush. It is said that when Gandhiji gifted a roll of this paper to Kaka Kalelkar, the Gujarati litterateur, he is known to have exclaimed, 'My pen is happy to write on this paper.' He used the Gujarati words 'kalam' for pen and 'khush' for happy, which when said together meant 'kalamkhush', and that is how this paper got its name.

It is made with flowers and grass petals. A pulp of waste and rags is mixed in a huge processor and later machine-pressed to the desired size, dried and prepared for the market. The same method is used to make paper with grass, coriander leaves, rice husk, jute, silk and flower petals. Colour is often added to make tinted, textured or marbled paper, which pays homage to Gandhiji's eco-friendly vision.

Opposite the ashram, there is a small home-based centre of organic food and a little ahead there is Sabarmati Jail, which has become known for its spicy fenugreek fritters mixed in a batter of chickpea, deep-fried and sold by the prisoners. They also have a counter there for yardage and biscuits.

If Gandhi Ashram is in one end of the city, situated along the river, Sarkhej Roza is in the opposite direction. Earlier, my home was on the way to Sarkhej Roza, which is one of the most beautifully landscaped mosques you will find and the ideological birthplace of Ahmedabad. Before I moved to my present home, I lived between Sarkhej Roza and the high-domed tomb of the architects of Ahmedabad, Azamkhan and Muazamkhan.

Most autorickshaw-wallahs, driving towards Vasna or Sarkhej, almost always stop at this Roza, to light agarbattis, and stand in silence with folded hands for a moment or two, before going on to their destination. It is said the Khan brothers had Persian lineage and were great archers. The tomb is erected on a raised plinth with corner bastions, and a staircase winds upwards from the entrance and leads to the terrace. This is more or less the only structure of its type in Ahmedabad and known to have similiarities to Mughal architecture with its double corridors like Humayun's Tomb in New Delhi. It is one of the earliest brick mausoleums of such size in Ahmedabad, like that of Darya Khan Ghummat in Shahibaug area, built around 1457.

At Sarkhej Roza, I am mystified by a silver chain which hangs from the high ceiling of Saint Sheikh Ahmed Khattu's tomb. The story of the chain came to me from various people, like autorickshaw-wallahs and the slipper keepers at the Roza. The thin line of this story is that they had an informal court at the Roza to question criminals. They were made to stand under the silver chain which was so long that it almost touched the grave of Ahmed Khattu. It was part of a ritual connected with passing judgement over convicts.

On the outside wall of this tomb, women tie colourful strings and bangles on the trellis, as they ask for the boon of a child. Once the wish is fulfilled, the infant is brought to the tomb and weighed in a scale, with an equal amount of sweets.

The silver chain no longer touches the floor and nobody knows when exactly the silver chain receded upwards. According to one story, some thieves tried to steal it, but as soon as they reached for it, the chain formed a tight noose around them and pulled them upwards. When they cried for help, it unfurled and dropped them on the floor. They were captured and punished for their crime. Since then the chain has been inaccessible and nobody dares to touch it.

In 1618, when Shah Jahan was governor of Gujarat, he was impressed by the monuments of Ahmedabad and became interested in their architecture. These monuments were built during the reign of Sultan Ahmed Shah in the early fifteenth century, which is known as the Sultanate period.

Ahmedabad was then known as Ashaval or Ashapalli, the third largest city of Gujarat after Patan, which was then the capital of Gujarat. The region on which Ahmedabad now stands was known as Ashaval after Asho Bhil, ruler of Gujarat in the eleventh century. But, when he was overpowered by Raja Karnadeva Solanki, Ahmedabad came to be known as Karnavati.

The Solanki period came to an end when Sultan Nasiruddin Mohamed bin Tughluq of the Delhi Sultanate dynasty conquered Gujarat and appointed Muzaffar Shah I as governor and established an independent kingdom in 1407. His grandson Ahmed Shah gave a cultural identity to Gujarat and shifted the capital from Patan to Ahmedabad.

After Ahmed Shah's death, Mohamed Shah I came to power, followed by Qutbuddin Ahmed Shah II and Abu Al Fatah Mehmud Shah, known as Begada, who conquered the fortresses of Champaner and Girnar and became a powerful ruler. He completed the fortification of Ahmedabad, which eventually came to be known as the walled city. There are many myths and legends about Begada. He liked to sit on the terrace of Teen Darwaza and watch the city. The step wells he built were classic examples of underground storage of rainwater. With all his eccentricities, Begada came to be known as a warrior and architect of Ahmedabad's fort walls and darwazas, the magnificent Adalaj step well, the pillared mosque of Rani Sipri, along with other mosques, mausoleums, forts and step wells of Gujarat. Before his death, he also expanded Sarkhej Roza by building palaces and extending the tank. According to his wish, he was buried at Sarkhej Roza, so that his soul could remain close to the resting place of saint Sheikh Ahmed Khattu.

The Sultanate period came to an end when Emperor Akbar conquered Gujarat in 1573. In 1753 Ahmedabad came under the joint rule of Mughals and the Maratha rulers Raghunath Rao Peshva and Damaji Gaekwad. But, when a conflict arose

between the Peshvas of Poona and Gaekwads of Baroda in 1818, the British East India Company conquered the city after the third Anglo-Maratha war.

Later, Mahatma Gandhi, decided to start the freedom movement from Ahmedabad and set up the ashram. The rest is history.

According to legend, Ahmed Shah wanted to build the city on the banks of the Sabarmati. It is said he saw a stray dog sniffing and rummaging among the burrows on the river bed, to feed upon young animals, when a wild hare rushed out and attacked him. The hare chased the dog, fighting it and driving it out of the vicinity. Ahmed Shah was surprised by its spirit and decided that he would build a city right there and name it Ahmedabad. Since then, there is a saying: 'Jab kutte par sassa aya, tab Ahmed Shah ne shehar basaya.'

Maybe, Ahmedabad has nothing to do with Teja, the beautiful Bhil princess, a dog and a hare, but more to do with the spiritual experience of a few people who conceived the city, which owes its existence to the Sufi saint Sheikh Ahmed Khattu, also known as Ganj Baksh, meaning bestower of wealth.

Ahmedabad was conceived in Saint Ahmed Khattu's magical mind. In 1337, he was born in Delhi, but later travelled to Rajasthan, as he was influenced by the Sufi saint Baba Ishaq. There he acquired mystical powers.

Khattu's camp resounded with music and poetry as he transformed it into a multi-faith centre for people of all communities. He was invited by Zaffar Khan, governer of Patan, who requested him to stay back in Gujarat. He accepted the invitation and after exploring the land, settled down in Sarkhej, a suburban village, near present-day Ahmedabad, which was known for its indigo farming.

Sultan Ahmed Shah was Khattu's follower and sought his advice for laying the foundation of the city. Khattu told him to find four religious men with proven piety, all named Ahmed, to lay the foundation stone of the city. He also asked him to invite twelve righteous men, known as Bavas, to consecrate the city's foundation.

The sultan found four Ahmeds for the ceremony in 1411. Ahmed Shah stood facing east, Saint Sheikh Ahmed Khattu faced west, Kaji Ahmed faced north and Mullah Malik Ahmed faced south.

The four Ahmeds laid the foundation stone of Ahmedabad near the old town of Ashaval on the eastern side of the river at Maneck Burj. In 2010, when the Ahmedabad Municipal Corporation celebrated six hundred years of the city's existence, the twelfth descendant of Saint Manecknath hoisted a white, green and saffron flag in memory of their ancestor's confrontation with Sultan Ahmed Shah during Dussehra, the tenth day of Navratri, symbolic of Lord Rama's victory over the demon king Ravana.

In ancient times, when the tank at Sarkhej Roza was full of rainwater, it had crocodiles and waterbirds. This beautiful architectural unit is spread out on about thirty-two acres of land with palaces, tombs, tanks, mosques and trees. It has Muslim, Hindu and Jain principles, known as the Saracenic form of architecture with ringed domes, pillars, courtyards and stone traceries that create a beautiful play of light and shadows in the Roza. The construction of the entire Sarkhej Roza was completed in 1458. A few years back, the Roza was in a dilapidated condition, but it is now being maintained by the Archaeological Survey of India and houses the Ganj Baksh Academic and Research Centre.

A high point of architecture from the Sultanate period in Ahmedabad is the Kankaria Lake or Hauz-e-Qutb. In AD 1415 Qutbuddin Ahmed Shah II started considering various sites to build a lake near Ahmedabad. He saw a range of hillocks and threw a pebble or kankar in a low-lying area between the hillocks and asked his engineers to dig a lake in that very place and name it Kankaria. It is a polygon with thirty-four sides with cut-out stone steps and an inlet sluice and circular openings on the eastern side with a summer palace in the centre of the lake. Another version is that there was a drought in Gujarat and the lake was built to sustain the poor people of the city.

Another Sufi saint connected with the history of Ahmedabad is Pir Mohammad Shah, who lived in Ahmedabad during the rule of Aurangzeb. He possessed an extraordinary power of memorizing religious texts. During his lifetime, he amassed a huge collection of manuscripts and books of great spiritual value. These were housed in the 'Qutubkhana' or library, which is one of the oldest libraries in India with a collection of original manuscripts in Arabic, Persian, Urdu, Sindhi and Turkish.

The library has wooden furniture, old fans and a tall glass case, where a huge candle from the Sultanate period is preserved. A copy of Mona Lisa on the wall has an Urdu inscription, 'This is Mona Lisa with her famous smile.' The library is known to host mushairas by the Muslim Writers Academy. An old black-and-white photograph on the wall shows well-known poets like Kaifi Azmi, Majrooh Sultanpuri, Ramanand Sagar, Waris Alvi and others, who came to the city for mushairas when they were young and unknown. In another room, technicians from Delhi have digitized ancient manuscripts.

This library is in a lane of shoe shops, a single-screen theatre which shows Gujarati films and a popular fruit juice centre, known as 'Mehndi Rang Lagyo', named after a popular Gujarati film of the 1950s. It was one of the first roadside cafes of

Ahmedabad and people flocked there to see the processor imported from Germany.

Shah-e-Alam Roza in the far eastern suburbs of Ahmedabad is the only mosque in the city where, according to local residents, there is a grave of a washerwoman. It is an unusual story. Her name is not known, but according to legend, she was barren and asked the Sufi saint Shah Alam (1475–1575) and his brother for the boon of a child. Eventually, her wish was granted. But there was a hitch, as Shah Alam had granted her a son and his brother blessed her with a daughter. So, whenever she went to pay her respects to Shah Alam, the child transformed into a boy. The washerwoman was worried about her child's future and begged Shah Alam to give the child a male gender, which he granted. Later, this child took up his mother's profession and is buried next to her. These graves are on the way to the mosque of Shah Alam.

This campus has two mausoleums, a mosque and an assembly hall, while the inner chamber is pillared and has richly carved marble screens. Shah Alam's mosque is situated in a dense area, where every other ancient structure is used as a chicken coop, tea stall or cellphone store, and can be reached after crossing Sardar Bridge, Behrampura Circle and Kankaria Lake.

Built like a fortress, the massive green-and-yellow façade of the mosque has seven arches, which lead to a vaulted reservoir used for ablutions, while the flooring is made with an appealing combination of black, white and grey marble. The domed mosque with its magnificent stone tracery is embellished with inlay work and has tall minarets on both sides of the mosque.

Ahmedabad is best known for the paper kites, which are made in almost all areas of the city from Shah-e-Alam to Sarangpur,

Raipur, Tankshal, almost all streets of the walled city and suburban Juhapura. During Uttarayan, the kite-flying festival, Ahmedabadis can be seen flying kites all over the city with shouts of 'Kaipo Che . . .'

Kite making is a craft which is passed on from one generation to another. Ahmedabad is best known for its international kite-

flying festival, which has become one of the biggest events in the world. The venue is the Sabarmati river front, and kite fliers from Japan, China, France, Belgium, Germany, America and England gather on the plazas between Nehru Bridge and Gandhi Bridge. But, there are rules and regulations at the festival, like the compulsory use of nylon or plastic thread and a ban on paper kites and strings prepared with a paste of glass powder.

This synthetic wonderland of kites creates a panorama of innumerable shapes, geometric or those of human figures, birds and animals, or of Superman, Batman and a giant Hanuman. Flying thousands of kites attached to one string is a highlight of this festival.

A day before the festival, a visit to the kite market in the old city is a must at Tankshal Ni Pol, the wholesale kite market. It is a shopper's delight. They have everything from kites, strings, masks, cheap goggles, baby binoculars, home-made glue to stick torn kites, whistles, plastic trumpets, sport caps and candles for lanterns, used for flying kites at midnight.

Something or other is always happening in Ahmedabad, one highlight being the spectacular procession or nagar yatra of Lord Jagannath, his brother Balabhadra and sister Subhadra in their chariots. The presiding deity, Lord Jagannath, leaves his sanctum sanctorum and travels around the city in his chariot, followed by Balabhadra and Subhadra. Lord Jagannath is worshipped as an incarnation of Lord Vishnu, preserver and conserver of the universe.

For years, this procession has been following a definite route in the walled city. It has akhadas with acrobats and martial artistes from various organizations, winding through the narrow lanes of the old city, by foot, or on trucks or floats with tableaux

of Lord Jagannath's life. For those who follow the procession, there are many resting places along the way, hosted by welcome committees, where canopies are constructed for devotees to pause and enjoy a festive meal of puris, vegetables, samosas, along with ghee-soaked sweets like mohanthal, an all-time favourite with Ahmedabadis.

Elephants lead the procession and are painted in bright floral designs a day before by their mahouts or sadhus in a large open-air stable opposite the temple. The day before, devotees donate cash, almonds, dates, dried figs and lentils. Volunteers help in the kitchen by chopping, cutting, dicing kilos of figs and almonds for the khichdi, which is made in pure ghee with four types of pulses and rice, as it is supposed to be Lord Jagannath's favourite meal.

Mahant Dileepsinghji Maharaj, the head priest of the temple, leads the procession into the walled city, as a flower sprinkler showers the chariots with roses and marigold flowers. Dileepsinghji sits majestically in an open jeep, blessing the crowds with raised hands. He is a small, thin man with big flashing eyes. His long hair is tied in a topknot, and he has a flowing beard. He wears a rosary of rudraksha beads around his neck. He addresses the press and sends across the message of communal harmony to the people of Ahmedabad. Muslim leaders greet him with flowers and a silver replica of Lord Jagannath's chariot. He accepts it gracefully and hands it over to his attendants as rose sherbet is served to one and all.

The chariots are decorated with flowers and painted with pictures of Lord Jagannath, who appears in a log of wood and so has an abstract bird-beak-like black face with big, wide-open eyes. Balabhadra has a white face and Subhadra's is yellow. Lord Jagannath wears a green-gold flared skirt and a fan-shaped turban with gold ornaments, Balabhadra wears blue and Subhadra is draped in a red sari.

Their eyes are covered, as they are supposed to have eyesores, having eaten too many mangoes. So, mangoes of all shapes and sizes cover the temple floor like an artistic design. Later, their eye patches are removed, before they start their journey around the city. Lord Jagannath's maternal home is a temple in Luhar Ni Pol, which has an anteroom covered with silk curtains and is kept closed behind silver-plated doors.

If leaders of the Muslim community welcome the chariot procession of Lord Jagannath, in a similar way, during Muharram, when the tazia procession reaches Electricity House on Relief Road, the head priest of Jagannath temple gifts a silver memento to the leader of the Tazia Committee.

Most of the artisans who make tazias during Muharram, which are also known as days of mourning, live around the queen's tomb at Rani No Hajiro, Jamalpur, Dariapur and Kalupur. Tazias are miniature replicas of the mosque in Iraq of martyr Hazrat Imam Hussein ibn Ali, grandson of Prophet Mohammed.

The bamboo structures of tazias are embellished with shimmering coloured paper with cut-out designs. The workmanship is done with great precision, to make the tazia look like a real mosque. Lately, some artisans use computer-aided designs to decorate the tazias. Modern technical devices are also used, so that a tazia can shrink or expand according to the size of streets. The artisans who construct a tazia are different

from those who decorate it, wipe it clean and carry it. Often, the pious brush the tazias with peacock-feather brooms and light camphor to purify the atmosphere around it.

Raikhad's Bada Imamwada, near Gaekwad Ni Haveli, houses a beautiful tazia, made in 1984. It is covered with bronze, nickel, white copper, silver and gold leaf, so that it resembles a real mosque with double levels and a dome. An antique silver tazia made in memory of Imam Hussein's sister is displayed in a glass window and can be seen from the street, along with a leather water bottle, as Imam Hussein and his followers were denied water before they were beheaded.

A Hindu family has also been making tazias during Muharram since the last eighty years and joins in the procession, singing funeral songs in Gujarati, as Muslim women narrate the battle of Karbala.

Tazias are numbered by the Tazia Committee so that order is maintained as the procession winds through the walled city. It also ensures safe journey of the tazias with a posse of policemen. All along, free water and sherbet are served as a form of piety, while brass bands play plaintive tunes, and gymnasts, drummers, percussionists and camel carts accompany the procession. Men beat their chests and grieve during the procession and create a funeral-like atmosphere. Self-flagellation is also part of grieving, as bare-chested men whip themselves with hooked metal chains, tube lights and swords. The procession is surrounded by men carrying poles with green flags, which have symbols of the crescent moon and star. Often, a white horse decorated with embroidered trappings and flowers leads the procession, as after Imam Hussein's death, his horse returned back without him. Some tazias are often placed on wheels, rolled out on the night of Karbala and immersed in the river at Khanpur gate.

From Raikhad, a winding road leads to the new Expressway. I was told that there were emu farms near Ahmedabad, along Expressway No. 1, the quickest way to reach Vadodara and return the same day. Some office-goers commute between the two cities on a daily basis. The Expressway starts from the far eastern side of Ahmedabad, which is a rather shabby and chaotic industrial area, with low cost housing societies, inhabited by people who work in the unorganized sector of the city. As a child, I had seen hollowed ostrich and emu eggs as family heirlooms in the showcase of our home, and I had often wondered if it was possible to transform eggs of big birds into food.

We were on the outskirts of the city looking for these farms, when I heard the call of emus. The farms were built on infertile fields allotted to emu farmers as these big birds were now listed

as poultry under the Poultry Farm Registration and Regulatory Authority Act. In 2008, Gujarat entered the field of emu farming and soon Ahmedabad had more than fourteen emu hatcheries. Their droppings and egg shells were sold to farmers as manure, and oil was extracted from their fat.

It was diffcult to enter the farm as the cellphone of the owner was still switched off. The farm was guarded by Dobermanns and Rottweilers, so I kept a distance from the main gate.

It was getting dark and I was disappointed that I could not get close to them. There were open-air aviaries with the big birds calling out to each other and walking around with their awkward gait. The advertisement had mentioned the sale of emu chicks, so I was sure they also had emu eggs. I had heard that emu flesh was available for the table for a price, though maybe not in Ahmedabad.

We drove through a grove of ancient banyan trees on the outskirts of the city to another emu farm. The trees were tall and huge, maybe more than a hundred years old. They were large with canopies close to each other, so that sunlight could not enter, and the entire stretch was dark and cool even in the height of summer. The tree trunks were gnarled, twisted, hollowed and rose like towers into the sky, as their aerial roots descended from the branches and penetrated the earth, creating another forest. It was difficult for the taxi driver to skirt the trees and reach the emu farm.

The project had started on an enthusiastic note, but it was not successful and most emu farms closed down in Ahmedabad and the birds were sent to Animal Help Foundations.

1979—Vasna Gaam. I always thought we were going to live in Shahibaug forever, but that was not to be. Laxmi Nivas was on a hundred-year-old lease and as soon as it was over, the trustees of the Swaminarayan religious sect bought the land to build a temple along with a mall. As soon as the deal was done, Laxmi Nivas and all the houses around it had to be demolished and we had to leave.

That was also the year when I lost my mother. Father had already bought land in a green zone near Vasna, closer to Juhapura, far away in west Ahmedabad, where he built a small farmhouse, hoping to start kennels and a poultry farm when he retired from the zoo he had built around Kankaria Lake with the Ahmedabad Municipal Corporation.

When we lived there, the communal riots of 2002 changed the face of Ahmedabad. In 1970, Juhapura was not fully inhabited, but a wasteland between Vasna village and Sarkhej Roza. Here, poor migrants, daily wage workers and drought-hit people often made temporary shacks with plastic sheets, with the sky as a roof, till they found alternative accommodation in one of the many slums around the city or along the Sabarmati river bed. More recently, these have been shifted to the far eastern suburbs to realize the Sabarmati River Front Project.

The Sabarmati was always temperamental, flooding during monsoons, but generally dry and often used as a cricket ground by youngsters, a temporary circus ground, or for cultivating a vegetable patch, during the long summer months. Cloth dyers and dhobis also used the river water, and sand merchants brought their donkeys to the river bed for transporting sand, while herons waded around them and buffaloes soaked in patches of shallow water.

In 1973 the Sabarmati flooded and carried away huts of the slum dwellers living along it, leaving many homeless, and the government decided to make low-cost housing for those who were displaced. The colony was built on a wasteland and named Sanklitnagar. Homes were allotted to people of all communities, to foster communal harmony.

I cannot place a finger on a particular date or year and say when exactly Sanklitnagar became Juhapura, a Muslim settlement. With every communal riot in Ahmedabad, the Muslim community felt safer in the homes of their relatives living in Juhapura and started buying the tenements owned by Hindus at low prices. Another Muslim neighbourhood was near Sarkhej Roza, where they lived along with Hindu families in Makarba village. Besides, some Hindu families who had lived along the river for years preferred to return there and rebuild the homes they had left behind after the floods.

During the riots of 2002, most Muslim families moved to Juhapura, making it a stronghold of the Muslim community. More recently, a road has been built from this area leading to Vejalpur, where a wall separates Hindu and Muslim areas. The wall has become symbolic of the great divide between both communities there. Some Muslim families still continue to live in the communally sensitive areas of Dariapur, Delhi Gate, Khanpur, Mirzapur and Kalupur, but also have houses in Juhapura, where they shift whenever there is any rumour of trouble.

Beyond Sarkhej and the new Ring Road, new industries have been allotted land. This is also where the corporate world has its elite townships. In a way, if Juhapura has encircled the Sarkhej–Vejalpur belt, it is also surrounded by these industries and housing colonies. So, in principle, almost everybody working and living on the Sanand highway has to pass through Juhapura.

Those who understand the meaning of a ghetto and the implications of chaotic urban planning, dread to think of the consequences if Ahmedabad were to have another communal riot. Unlike before, Juhapura is now self-sufficient with its own schools, hospitals, malls, shops and even a dairy, so it is better equipped to face a curfew or other restrictions during a riot.

High-rise apartment buildings, along with housing societies, surround Juhapura, extending towards Sarkhej Roza. Most buildings, row houses and tenements are in pastel colours with distinct Islamic features like arches or minarets, complete with symbols of crescent moon and star.

It is a well-known fact that most craftspeople live here and the janoi or the sacred thread worn by Brahmins is made here. This is also where most autorickshaw-wallahs live. Often they change their name when they ply their vehicles during communal riots and are usually known as Babu, Pappu or Raju. It is an area with which I have some connection, as I said. Near Juhapura, we had another family house, where we lived for twenty-five years. We moved into this house after leaving Shahibaug. It had one big living room, a veranda, kitchen-cum-dining room, a garden and a bedroom upstairs wih a terrace, from where we could see the fields behind the house. Ours was the only minority house, crammed between a Hindu village, Vasna, and a Muslim settlement, Juhapura.

There were slums in the street across our house which had a mixed population of Dalits, Thakores who worked as farmers, rabaris belonging to a cowherd community, Muslims and Rajasthani sand traders who kept donkeys and trucks for transporting sand to construction sites. The road around the house was often jammed with donkeys, cows, buffaloes and camels which belonged to various communities who lived around our house. Our driver Ahmedbhai, also lived there and told us that his house was cool during summer months, as it was built on an old step well. According to him, a pair of cobras lived there and sometimes emerged in his kitchen and returned to the well. Nobody was harmed. We did not believe him, till the step well was discovered by a French renovation architect and this place became known as a heritage site.

As we settled into the new house, my father built one more room on the terrace and covered every possible wall in the house with antiques, paintings, photographs and trophies of birds and animals. We also had Pekinese dogs and a talking parakeet for company. Besides, many birds came to the garden as the house was in close proximity to the river. Slowly, all this was to change, after my father's death. By then, the house was encroached upon by another slum, which was getting bigger and more dangerous after every communal riot. Muslims sold their houses to Hindu neighbours and settled down in Juhapura.

During the riots of 2002, Muslims of the walled city took refuge in Juhapura; but for that, they had to drive through a road running next to our house, which became the scene of the worst massacres seen in Ahmedabad. A year before the riots, we had had a traumatic experience when Gujarat was jolted by an earthquake. These are notes that I wrote about the earthquake followed by the communal riots of 2002.

Ahmedabad—*24 January 2001*

My daughter, son-in-law and six-month-old grandson had arrived from Paris to spend time with me. My son was also there. The night before, I was happy that we were all together.

For many years, my son-in-law has often come to India, but never travelled to Kutch. So, on the twenty-second night he took a luxury bus to Bhuj, with plans to stay there for two days and return on the twenty-sixth. Instead, he came back to Ahmedabad on the twenty-fifth night.

26 January 2001

We woke up at 8 a.m. The koel was calling frantically and I assumed we would have an early monsoon. The koel made Lassie, our pet canine, nervous. She was barking and running the entire length and breadth of the garden. Her barking affected Gangaram, our plum-headed parakeet, sitting in his cage, which I had hung on the branch of a chikoo tree. He was screeching as if he had seen a falcon. I looked out of the kitchen window and saw a flock of rosy pastors flying out of the tree and frightening the squirrels.These mad flutters scared a sunbird, which entered the kitchen from the half-open back door. I thought I should go to the backyard and see what was happening, but before that I needed a cup of tea.

At 8.46, I was making tea when I heard a water tanker pass by the house; my hand trembled as I poured the tea into the kettle. But, the house continued to shake even after the tanker passed. We knew this was different and looked at each other, worried. We could hear something like a roar; the kitchen floor seemed to be moving, as if there was a dragon running under the floor. It was hard to maintain our balance. Yet, I ran upstairs to wake up my son. We ran into each other and realized that it was an earthquake. The family rushed out of the house and stood in the open, as the roads and open grounds were filling with people. It was a monstrous earthquake with its epicentre in Kutch.

Innumerable people had died and many people were trapped in flats, which had been razed to the ground all over Gujarat.

27 January

The house was damaged. There were cracks everywhere. The beam of my bedroom seemed to sag over my head and we decided to sleep downstairs. The news of the earthquake had reached all over the world and the telephone did not stop ringing.

30 January 2001

With a heavy heart, I left my daughter and her family at the Sardar Vallabhbhai Patel International Airport.

A year later, 30 January 2002

The house in Vasna was situated on the border, between a Muslim area, Juhapura, and a Hindu settlement, Vasna gaam. Between the two, mine was the only Jewish house. I felt as though I was caught between the hateful warp and weft of two communities. The worst scenes of the riots were seen here and just one incident changed everything for me.

But, it took me five more years to leave the house. It is never easy to leave a family home. Ahmedabad is now a divided city. A journalist friend once said that there are two Ahmedabads, like two cities in one, a Hindu Ahmedabad and a Muslim Ahmedabad.

28 February 2002

After the train was burnt at Godhra and the bodies arrived in Ahmedabad, there were communal riots in the city. And, in the street across my house, I saw mobs with weapons, killing, looting, plundering, shouting, screaming, violating women as columns of fire rose over the city. That is when, sitting at my computer, behind locked doors, I wrote the poem, 'Long Night of the Unsheathed Sword'. The day after, I started a novel titled *The Man with Enormous Wings* where I created an imaginary Mahatma Gandhi returning to Ahmedabad and trying to stop the riots. Today, all is well in 'Vibrant Gujarat'. Yet, as it always happens, Ahmedabad will again see another communal riot. We have always had riots, which created illusionary walls between people. These have now become real walls.

December 2007

I sold the house and bought an apartment in upmarket west Ahmedabad. When I left the house, the trees had grown taller

than the house, their girth so enormous that I could not encircle them with both my hands. The interior of the house was like a cocoon—cool, dark and inviting. I could never adjust to my new surroundings, till I discovered Gulmohar flats.

At Gulmohar, I can breathe easy, as my neighbours are largely non-vegetarian and fragrances of curries float from one apartment to the other, similar to our old homes in Delhi Gate and Shahibaug. On Saturdays, they go shopping for the weekly quota of chicken, fish, mutton and eggs. At Gulmohar, Sparky, a stray dog, came into my life, although I had decided not to keep pets, as I had lost many in the last few years.

In Ahmedabad, pedigreed dogs have always been kept as pets and guard dogs by mill owners, government officers, royal families, Anglo-Indians, Christians, Parsis, Jews, or foreigners settled in Gujarat, but keeping a stray dog as a pet was unheard of. They were for the street. At some point, a white spitz, which looked like a medium Pomeranian, started featuring in Hindi films and suddenly, a largely vegetarian Gujarat woke up to the fact that pedigreed dogs could be kept as pets and fed vegetarian food.

So far, dogs were always associated with non-vegetarianism. Soon, there were many people looking for a Pamariyu, meaning a Pomeranian, which was not expensive, like some other pedigreed dogs. Keeping pet dogs became a craze after the release of the blockbuster Bollywood film *Hum Aapke Hain Koun*, where the toy-like dog Tuffy plays a pivotal role in the happy ending of the film. If the film's wedding rituals caught the fancy of the nation, Tuffy entered Gujarati homes. He became part of the drawing room furniture, fattening on dal, rice, chapattis, Gujarati snacks, leftovers and ice cream. And, if Tuffy lived in an apartment, he waited for the precious evening outing, when the women or children took a walk with their dog in the local municipal garden. Tuffy was no longer non-vegetarian, so much so that once in a while even a conservative grandmother threw a biscuit at the dog, as long as it did not clamber over her or enter the puja room. By the way, male or female, most pet dogs were known as Tommy. Slowly the doggy scene of Ahmedabad changed.

In Gujarat, 'sheri na kutra' literally means street dogs, as stray dogs always guard certain areas where they are fed. In the process, Ahmedabad has large packs of stray dogs. Their taste buds are used to regular Gujarati food, along with pizzas, pasta and noodles. 'Dog-dom' or the kingdom of stray dogs has increased manifold in the city. The adage that a dog is a human being's best friend stands true in most cases, but lately stray dogs are in the news almost every day. They are everywhere, and specialize in terrorizing people riding two-wheelers, specially late at night. Dog packs are very smart, because, as soon as they see the municipal van, which arrives with dog catchers and butterfly nets, they instinctively abandon their regular territories and disappear into nowhere. While doing their Houdini act, they vent such strange wails that all the other dogs in the entire area too turn tail. So, the municipal staff can hardly catch a dog or two. As soon as the van disappears around the corner, the packs are back at their regular posts. While Ahmedabadis encourage stray dogs in their areas, they do not take an interest in their health problems, nor do they cooperate with authorities to get them sterilized. When these dogs get attached to some families, they are not given names or collars, so that municipal

ESTHER DAVID

officials may not know that they belong to a certain person or housing societies. We also feed langurs, even if they enter our kitchens and scare us. Feeding stray animals is part of our country's great recycling system.

In Ahmedabad, the Tuffy era did not last long, though they are still seen in some homes. Other breeds are in vogue, like Dobermanns, Alsatians, golden retrievers, beagles, Dalmatians and pugs, which became prize pets after a well-known telecom company's commercial was aired on television.

For all the fascination with dogs as pets, there is a downside too. After the initial enthusiasm, when pedigreed dogs were sold at high prices, the pet scene turned bleak. There were reports about cruelty to animals. Often, dogs were abandoned by their owners and found roaming aimlessly in the city. Some owners left their pets at animal help foundations when they were travelling and never returned to take their pets back home. Other cases were reported of owners leaving dogs locked up in their balconies with very little water and food. Neighbours heard their pitiable howling till the owners returned.

Animal lovers were in for a bigger shock when an African grey parrot was found injured and flapping its wings on busy C.G. Road, till a kind animal activist took it home, where it settled down in a makeshift cage and greeted them in French with 'Bonjour'. They issued an announcement in the papers, but nobody came to claim the bird.

As these stories seeped into the press, there was a sudden spurt of NGOs and animal help foundations which offered various free-of-cost facilities to citizens, like capturing serpents from housing societies, saving birds during kite-flying festivals, sterilizing stray dogs and providing shelter for unwanted pets or stray animals and birds. For years, I followed these stories, but did not take active interest in what was happening around me, till Sparky came into my life in the most unexpected way.

When I moved out from my bungalow in Vasna to a ninth-floor apartment in the posh Satellite area. I could not settle down and in a year I rented it out to a corporate and bought a ground floor apartment from my cousin, who lives in Canada and had decided to sell it. This apartment was in one of the last surviving Parsi colonies of the city.

It had spacious rooms, high ceilings, large windows and doors which opened into an empty space, where I planned to have a small garden. This is where I met Sparky, a stray puppy, which had been run over by a speeding car and broken his foreleg. So, he took refuge in a flower bed close to my flat. We named him Sparky.

Sparky's leg was swollen and he was in pain. So, we called an animal help foundation with an apt name, Asha. They arrived in an hour, dressed his wound, applied medicine, injected painkillers and gave him some precautionary shots. This condition lasted for more than fifteen days, till one day, we noticed that his leg had putrefied and there were maggots in the wound. Sparky was dying. It was suggested that his leg should be amputated as his survival was at stake. We agreed to save him at all costs. He was taken to an animal hospital and his leg was amputated. We were told that the surgery had been a success. Sparky was courageously responding to post-operative care and recovering fast.

A month later, a three-legged Sparky was back with us. Spunky Sparky had learnt to live on three legs instead of four and had accepted his tripod condition. He also learnt that instead of limping, it was easier to run on threes and get around the place. Today, Sparky is the centre of our lives. He is fed bread with milk and receives a special Sunday lunch of meat dishes, but does not care for vegetables. He wears a Swiss collar, a tick belt with a bell and some chewy toys. He takes commands and is toilet-trained; so he does not pee or poo on the landings of Blocks A and B.

Sparky has created territorial rights around the flats and chases away other strays and barks at strangers. He feels safe in these premises and once in a while fearlessly ventures out of the gates, but never leaves the compound after 8 p.m., when he prefers to sit near the watchman. He has become an excellent guard dog, so much so that people hesitate to enter the flats unannounced. And, when the watchman is on leave, he automatically becomes our guardian, keeping awake all night and giving warning signals when he hears untoward night sounds, so half-asleep we speak to him, even if it is words like, 'Sparky, shut up.'

Like all domestic animals, the process of humanization has started. Sparky is happy when we are all at home, have holidays or the children have a vacation. He loves to run after them when they play football, cricket or cycle around the flats. But other cyclists are not allowed.

On hot afternoons, he sleeps in the flower beds, and nights are spent on my doormat. Even with three legs, he is agile, chases strays and digs up my precious flower beds. But he never enters my ground-floor apartment, even if the door is open. Fortunately, he does not mind being leashed, but hates water and we cannot wash him. Sparky's community adoption has many advantages, because if you have a dog at home, it can restrict your movements. With Sparky, however, there are no problems, as he belongs to all of us, and somebody is always there to look after him. Quietly, he has entered our lives and made a place in our hearts. Because, it is all about love me, love my dog.

Then, when Sparky was five years old, he fell in love. One day in the monsoon he disappeared for two days, only to return tired and hungry. He was followed by a female of his species, much smaller in size than him.

I had often seen her in the street in the company of other male dogs and I could see from the scratches on Sparky's body that he had fought bloody battles with bigger dogs, just to win his lady-love. We named her Mandy. On the first day, Sparky was willing to share his food bowl with his new wife, but the day after, he did not want to share his food with her, so we fed her in a separate bowl. Since then, Mandy has moved in with Sparky and has quickly learnt the rules of living with us, proving that marriages are made in heaven.

If Ahmedabad has its own 'dog-dom', once we also had our own 'cow-land'. It was impossible to walk, cross roads or drive in the city until a few years back when stray cattle were herded into a cattle pound and their owners were fined if they allowed them to forage in the city. Ahmedabad is also going green, as the civic body has started a large-scale drive to plant trees in the city and provide trees to house owners or housing societies, if they ensure they will look after the trees.

Our housing society is surrounded by trees, yet silently I lament for the trees I have lost, while moving from one house to the other. Having lived in different parts of the city, I have seen that people have different attitudes towards trees. In the most unlikely places one can see a touch of green, as often vegetable vendors also grow tulsi outside their shops. Once, at Parimal Garden Nursery, while I was collecting saplings from the officer-in-charge, my autorickshaw-wallah took a sapling for his courtyard. As a rule, holy trees like banyan and peepal are always looked after well in India. Some architects in Ahmedabad are also known to design houses around trees, while some high-rise apartments have special parks of their own. There are private estates on S.G. Road, or Sarkhej–Gandhinagar highway, where they grow exotic herbs, lettuce or basil and flowers like geraniums. I envy people who live in lush-green surroundings like the IIM at Vastrapur and the National Institute of Design or NID at Paldi. These are green islands with lawns, gardens and trees, a virtual birdwatcher's paradise. Similar luxuriant green zones exist at the Centre for Environmental Planning and

Technology, known as CEPT University, Gujarat College, Gujarat University and Gujarat Vidyapeeth, which was started by Mahatma Gandhi.

I live in Ambawadi, which is almost at the centre of the city and set amidst bungalows with gardens. Before the city extended from old to new, Ambawadi was a mango orchard, as the name suggests. An educational campus here still has old mango trees, but mostly the trees were cut down to build apartments, housing societies and shopping centres. Yet, this area has two public gardens, overgrown with magenta bougainvillea creepers on the fence. My neighbour had a chikoo tree, which was eventually chopped down, and there is a jamun tree on my right. Gulmohar trees are seen inside and outside the colony, along with neem trees; and Rangoon creepers along with curtain veils fall gracefully on the boundary walls of most housing societies. One can watch parakeets, bulbuls, robins, tailorbirds, sunbirds, common green bee-eaters, doves, mynahs, sparrows, munias, crow pheasants, Brahminy kites and other birds in the lush green foliage. At night, a colony of parakeets roosts on the awning of a tenth-floor apartment, so I wake up to their pleasant chattering.

The chikoo tree next door was framed in my bedroom window. One morning I heard great commotion and saw that it was being cut down. I was helpless, but I did not know the owner, so could not stop her. She said the tree attracted insects and langurs. I felt it was not enough reason to cut down a tree that took years to grow and would only take a couple of hours to chop down. By evening, the tree was no longer framed in my window; instead it had been lugged off as firewood by the sweeper woman's family.

A few days later, in a similar way, when the next-door

neighbour started cutting down a young neem tree, hesitantly I requested him to reconsider his decision, for that much-needed green cover, which was also a haven for birds.

I assumed, he would resent my interference, but much to my surprise, he stopped the operation. I heaved a sigh of relief that I could save a tree and start dreaming about a green future for Ahmedabad.

New Ahmedabad on the western side with its cosmopolitan community has come to terms with the availability of non-vegetarian food in the city. Rows of tempos are lined up along the wall of the IIM, selling poultry, goat meat and fresh fish

from the Department of Fisheries of the Gujarat government. Frozen food shops are popular too as they have ready-to-cook food, along with chicken, mutton, fish, pork, salami, ham, turkey and a variety of cheese.

But it is illegal to buy, sell or eat beef in the city. The state government passed the Gujarat Animal Preservation Act in 2011, whereby it amended the provisions of the Gujarat Animal Preservation Act of 1954. So, trade, storage and transport of beef or any of its products has been banned in the state. Buying or selling beef is a criminal offence in Ahmedabad. To prove this point, at Ambawadi Circle, there is a memorial to Geetaben Rambhia, considered to be a martyr, as she lost her life while fighting for the cause of banning beef in the city.

Ahmedabad is well known for its largely vegetarian population and has a few non-vegetarian restaurants. But, you will find many vegetarians who have converted to non-vegetarianism, though meat is rarely cooked at home. Instead, they eat tandoori or butter chicken at restaurants or at Bhatiyar Gully, which is a favourite haunt for foodies.

Eggs were first accepted in Ahmedabad when enterprising vendors did brisk business by making spicy omelettes on their four-wheeler carts, which were seen all over the city. Eggs are whipped with minced onions, finely chopped green chillies, powdered spices and coriander leaves, and flip-fried in oil and served with tomato ketchup and butter-fried buns.

Unlike before, in Bhatiyar Gully, one sees families or groups of students eating chicken and paneer dishes together on the same table. In contrast, I have also met people who have an aversion to eggs and fish. Recently, a well-travelled friend beat a hasty retreat from a dinner party when he got the whiff of fish being fried in the host's kitchen.

In contrast, at the launch of a five-star hotel's food festival, they had a large vegetarian counter with pasta, a variety of cheese, sliced garlic bread, paneer butter masala, parathas and Gujarati street food, along with a smaller table for non-vegetarians with Singapore chicken curry with fried rice and a roasted leg of lamb. Surprisingly even as the chef sliced it, revealing the animal's thigh bone, there were no visible reaction of distaste from the vegetarian guests. So, perhaps the jet-setter Ahmedabadi is fast becoming more tolerant to meat dishes.

The only mystery is how on earth you can make the all-time favourite of Ahmedabadis, the Black Forest cake, without eggs. Maybe, when necessary, they turn a blind eye to eggs in cakes. Actually, I admire the innovative capabilities of our women,

who have created eggless cake, as it is supposed to be healthy and low in cholesterol. I remember, once I asked for garlic bread in a newly opened bakery and much to my chagrin, the man at the counter was offended and said it was an eggless bakery, meaning even garlic was taboo. A common Ahmedabadi joke is about vegetarian chicken, meaning chicken made without onion and garlic.

While researching for this book, I discovered that Ahmedabadis love fusion food, because they have extended families abroad and travel much more than before. Their food habits have changed as they experiment with recipes of other countries and mix them with Indian ingredients. Of course, once in a while, they revert back to traditional Gujarati food.

At wedding receptions in Ahmedabad, besides the camera cranes, I noticed this shift at wedding dinners during the 1990s, where it was fashionable to ask caterers to serve multi-cuisine fusion dinners, often along with a live dhokla or pasta counter.

Actually, non-Gujaratis refer to khaman dhokla in one breath, assuming that it is the same thing. Even in Hindi cinema or television serials, what is known as dhokla is khaman, which is yellow in colour and made with chickpea batter, while dhokla is fluffy white, steamed and made with rice and white lentils. During the last few years, it has received a new avatar, as it is made like a mini chutney sandwich. Both khaman and dhokla come under the category of farsan, meaning snacks served as accompaniments to regular food, without which a Gujarati thali or food platter is incomplete.

Ahmedabad is also well known as the ice cream capital of India. Blame it on the long summer months or innumerable ice cream centres all over the city or just that we have a sweet tooth and keep a close watch on advertisements and hoardings for the latest flavours of the season. Almost all the advertisements claim that these ice creams are vegetarian and this could be one reason ice cream is so popular in the city.

For years, I have experimented with Outsider Art and worked with children from the Devi Pujak or the tribal Vaghri community as they are an extremely talented people with unexplored creative energies. The response was so enthusiastic that I was taken by surprise. The clay modelling done by the almost naked children with runny noses reminded me of the clay figurines seen in the Indus Valley civilization. Let me add here that often, their parents helped them make the forms, but were shy to admit that as adults they had made toys. A form that really excited me was that of a bull standing with his hooves on a couple's shoulders. I knew that I could never have been able to do something so beautiful. The result was so good that I decided to fire these works at a potter's kiln. So, I started searching for a potter on the Sabarmati river bed.

This is where I met Lavingben. An illiterate, she was a widow with seven children, who made a living by recycling old gunny bags. The entrance to her house was decorated with brightly coloured tiger heads. During the festivals she sold colourful clay bowls, as she had learnt this craft from her grandfather. She made her own mixture with clay, paper, crystals of raw glue and fenugreek powder. Slowly, she started making animal and bird figurines and later took to making Ganesha sculptures. She was a natural artist.

Around this time, I discovered Devooben. While passing her

house in an autorickshaw, I saw a beautiful quilt hanging on the wall of her house. A mother of five, all daughters, she tried to give colour to her life through the memory of a childhood spent in Saurashtra. She had a highly interesting sense of design and colour. Then, I met Pushpa Rajaram in Juhapura at the community centre where I was working with Father Erewitti of the St Xaviers Social Service Scheme. Pushpa came to me, her face hidden in her veil, and asked me for work. 'What can you do?' I asked her.

'Nothing,' she said. I insisted that she speak to me without the veil. When she lifted it, the first thing I noticed was a finely drawn line of sindoor in her hair and the clean lines of kajal in her eyes. She had four children and a handicapped husband, who had lost his arm in an oil press. She needed to work and earn a living. I gave her some paper and asked her to paint. With the colours I had given her, she painted quickly, with a natural flair for line, colour and composition. Her favourite subject was Krishna. Each painting had a story. Pushpa started earning well by transferring her paintings into patchwork and bought two sewing machines. Her forays in the art world strengthened her and she no longer covered her face. She learnt to read and write and was respected in her society as an accomplished craftperson.

After the communal riots of 1988, I felt the need to communicate with the people living in the street across my house. Ahmedbhai, our family driver, belonged to the Langha community. He introduced me to the women of the hutments around my old house, where I introduced art as a form of development, which took me on another journey leading to the area of Outsider Art.

I am sentimental about the Sabarmati, as it was here that I

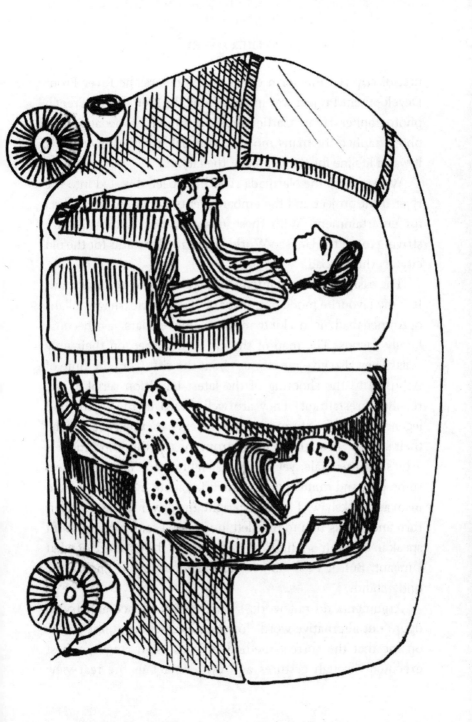

first discovered this form of art, much before the River Front Development Project was implemented. In 1966, famed French photographer Henri Cartier-Bresson was in Ahmedabad and photographed the many moods of the Sabarmati, showing that it was a lifeline for the people of the city.

Waters from the Narmada river have been diverted into the river front project and the embankments have become an area for entertainment. With these changes, civic authorities are striving to get the Unesco World Heritage City status for the old city of Ahmedabad.

The easiest way to go into the walled city is by autorickshaw. It is my favourite mode of transport. The autorickshaw-wallahs of Ahmedabad mean a lot to me and some regulars have become family friends. The map of the city is inscribed on their grey cells. They also give me stories about the city, from the time of Asho Bil to the shooting of the latest television serial at the revolving restaurant. They are well-versed in the myths and legends about the city and are storytellers par excellence. Maybe their stories are a little different from the real thing and there is a twist in their tale, yet it is never fabricated. They also have some plus and minus points, which fascinate me. While seated in an autorickshaw, if I say, turn right, the driver thinks it is a left turn and if I ask him to turn left, he is sure I said, turn right. If I speak in Gujarati or Hindi, he understands the opposite of what I meant. But, if I ask him to turn right or left in English, he understands.

Arguments do not work, so I keep my silence and try to figure out alternative words for simple directions, till it dawns on me that the correct method is to use sign language, best executed through gestures and eye contact in the rear-view mirror of the auto. This is when the gender issue rears its head as he sniggers at me with a look which says, women have no sense of roads. Then he relaxes, brakes with one foot and crossing his legs on the seat says, 'That road is closed; there is a traffic jam.' I have no other alternative but to sit back and hope to reach my destination in time.

Sometimes, I meet a daredevil auto-bhai, who, even when I am not in a hurry, drives at breakneck speed, vanquishing bigger vehicles, as my pleas to slow down fall on deaf ears. If I am in a hurry, he moves like a snail with excuses that his vehicle is in reserve or he has had family problems that very morning. All this can be handled as long as he does not give signals with his foot, sticking it out of the auto and moving it up and down.

Minus all these problems, he is a charmer, as while driving, some auto-bhais determine how friendly you are by studying you in the rear-view mirror, as they want to chat and tell you their life story, political views, or city stories. So far, they are known to be safe with women, even at night. Sometimes people of his fraternity are obliging, others are not, especially those near airports and railway stations are particularly difficult. So what if an auto-bhai has a language problem and even if he does make an extra U-turn or two, he may charge extra or even surprise you by asking for less on the grounds that it was his mistake, not yours, as the rate card is a sensitive issue, a matter of honour. And, when he drives like crazy, he will reassure you with a smile, 'Your life is as precious as mine.' I like to refer to them as my eccentric auto-bhais of Ahmedabad.

For years, they contributed to the pollution level of the city, when they ran on petrol. To add to the smog, when they were short of cash, some auto-bhais added kerosene to petrol and made things worse, till the new sleek, green, compressed natural gas or CNG autorickshaws arrived.

As a rule, autorickshaw-wallahs do not keep change. So the next best thing to do is carry a meter card and make sure that you have coins of two's and five's. It is difficult to understand the auto-wallahs' logic about these numbers. Maybe, it is something to do with luck.

I have had only one bad experience with an auto-bhai, while returning from the airport at 10 p.m. due to a late flight. I took an autorickshaw, not realizing that the driver was drunk and I had to get off halfway, bag and baggage. Since then, I make sure that a known auto-bhai is waiting for me at the airport. I also feel troubled when I am charged a hundred rupees instead of forty or when an auto-bhai stubbornly announces, 'Rickshaw nahin jayegi,' meaning the auto has a mind of her own and she will not go to a particular destination, as he has no control over her.

Auto-bhais are an unpredictable lot, so try face reading. Some autorickshaw-wallahs are difficult and will not stop, during rush hour, late evening or on a rainy day, as they appear to be going home in the opposite direction. But, if you do find one, give him an address and he will reach you to your destination. Some auto-bhais are literate and read newspapers or magazines. They are cool, reasonable and ready to wait, if you need to make a few stops on the way, as they sit there reading, while listening to their battery-operated radios. Actually most auto-bhais have mobile phones with loud ringtones and will respect your request to halt on the side of the road when they receive a call. And, if you have booked them for half a day, they will offer you a cup of tea at their favourite tea stall. They all have a preference for posters of film stars, like a sari-clad Kareena Kapoor or Katrina Kaif, which are pasted inside the auto, while the mudguards almost always have an image of Amitabh Bachchan in his *Coolie* avatar or a shirtless Salman Khan. I have had some of the most stimulating conversations with auto-bhais, who have given me some of my best city stories for this book.

ACKNOWLEDGEMENTS

Somnath Chatterjee for looking after my laptop while I was writing and editing this book.

Anand Zaveri for making it possible for me to work on this book at Swati Snacks, Ahmedabad.

Friends and strangers who told me city stories.